French Revolution's Golden Resurgence

Lisa T. Jones

TABLE OF CONTENTS

INTRODUCTION

A haunting image from the hysteria of the French Revolution marked the official ratification of the new French constitution, the *Fête de l'Unité de l'Indivisibilité de la République*.[1] Although officially advertised as a celebration of the unveiling of the new constitution, this festival "featured some of the most bizarre iconography."[2] The ceremony started at the Place de la Bastille, where proudly stood a sculpture designed by the famous Neoclassical artist Jacques-Louis David.[3] Interestingly, this statue was of "a bare-breasted Egyptian nature goddess"—that is, Isis, the head goddess of the ancient Egyptian pantheon—juxtaposed next to "a Fountain of Regeneration."[4] After paying homage to this revived image of the ancient Egyptian tradition, the procession eventually meandered down to the Place de la Révolution, "where emblems of royalty were burned beneath a statue of the goddess of Liberty."[5] To conclude the Republican festivities, the procession, composed of both the people and the deputies of the state, "swore an eternal oath to the Constitution" beneath the bare sky at the Champ de Mars.[6] This *fête* comprised an interesting mélange of images, considering this was no procession belonging to a Greco-Roman mystery religion, but a new "secular" religion of an "enlightened" republic.

As illustrated by the fête of the Federation, radical political leaders copied and reshaped ancient concepts, symbols, and religious rituals for the sake of creating a new state religion, designed to replace Catholicism in France, during the heyday of the French Revolution. With

---

[1] Dan Edelstein, *Terror of Natural Right: Republicanism, the Cult of Nature, and the French Revolution* (Chicago: University of Chicago Press, 2009), 180.

[2] Ibid.

[3] Ibid., 181.

[4] Ibid.

[5] Ibid.

[6] Ibid.

these elements from Classical antiquity, major Revolutionary figures, such as Maximilien Robespierre, repackaged pre-Christian religious traditions as a new "rational" and "natural" religious system for the French Republic. Following the Romantic philosophical cues of Jean-Jacques Rousseau, the new religions of the state would strip off the "superstition" of the Church and return man to a mythical golden age guided by general revelation. Officially outlawed in France in 1793, Christianity became a byword for backwardness, and the state equated it as the opposite of all things enlightened, as opposed to the pagan-influenced[7] traditions of the new state. This intense phase of the French Revolution illustrates the power of old ideas and how an anti-Christian government can marry paganism to the in vogue "natural" philosophy and tout this "new" amalgamated belief system as "rational."

Unfortunately, this sort of rationalized superstition would rear its ugly head again during the first half of the twentieth century in the Third Reich, highlighting the dangerous power of secularized state religion. The cultural historiography of Nazism has begun to explore the unholy brew of Occultism, mysticism, ancient pre-Christian traditions, mytho-history, and scientism in recent years. Historians, such as Peter Levenda, Nicholas Goodrick-Clarke, David Luhrssen, Bill Yenne, Christopher Hale, and Heather Pringle, have explored in the past twenty years this previously unexplored region of Nazi Germany's Theosophical-Darwinist religion. Previously, such topics as the influence of popular Occultism in National Socialism were the sole stomping grounds of pseudo-historians and conspiracy theorists. While these—to utilize litotes—not

---

[7] For the sake of this research's argument, "paganism" is the breadth of ancient, pre-Christian European religious practices, particularly those of Greco-Roman civilization. Due to paganism's influence upon Occultism, some pagan aspects can fall under the umbrella of "the occult," or "high Western esotericism" (i.e., hidden practices from Egyptian and Classical civilizations, of a pre-Christian nature, and usually practiced by learned persons, such alchemists, astrologers, necromancers, Hermeticists etc.---practices generally rejected in the modern Western worldview). For further information, please see Nicholas Goodrick-Clarke's introductory chapter in *The Western Esoteric Traditions: A Historical Introduction*, Paul Kléber Monod's introduction in *Solomon's Secret Arts: The Occult in the Age of Enlightenment*, and Michael York's first chapter of *Pagan Theology: Paganism as a World Religion*.

academic "researchers" still remain and spread their ideas in fringe publications and among

conspiratorial Internet subcultures, properly trained historians have separated myth from fact and

shed new light onto how fantastical the Nazis' religious beliefs were. Goodrick-Clarke's *The*

Occult Roots of Nazism: Secret Aryan Cults and Their Influence on Nazi Ideology, for example,

argues that Ariosophist[8] Occultism helped shape the Nazis' worldview, from the Nazis' ties to

Occult groups, such as the Thule Society, in the days before the failed Putsch to Heinrich

Himmler's obsession with all pre-Christian Germanic Odin-worship.[9]

As historians of Nazi Germany continue to explore the bizarre qualities of Nazi religious

culture, eighteenth-century historians continue to overall ignore the eccentricities of the French

Revolution's state cults. How dechristianization, the Cult of Reason, and the Cult of the Supreme

Being have not captured the imaginations of historians remains a mystery: the subject is too

fantastical and sensational not to research. In today's "publish or perish" academic culture; it is

amazing that historical researchers are not regularly churning out best-sellers about the cults; yet

the historiography remains overall threadbare.

The favored approaches to cultural histories of the French Revolution and the Republic

typically fixate upon elements such as the impact of the growing public sphere, Grub Street

publications, philosophical discourse or even Roger Chartier's pretentious thesis of the

---

[8] Ariosophy is a mystical ideology that combined *völkisch* nationalism, Aryan supremacy, and the esoteric teachings of Occult icon Helena Blavatsky. For more details, see Chapter 2 of Nicholas Goodrick-Clarke's *The Occult Roots of Nazism*.

[9] To briefly summarize and help provide further insight, Himmler injected his anti-Christian, Occult religious philosophy into his policies with the SS and the *Ahnerbe* (the Nazis' bureau of archaeological research). To name a few examples, Himmler patronized a Wotanist seer (Karl Maria Wiligut) as his official SS researcher of Aryan prehistory and ordered the *Ahnerbe* to videotape witches who claimed to be mediums in contact with pre-historic Aryans. See Bill Yenne's *Hitler's Master of the Dark Arts: Himmler's Black Knights and the Occult Origins of the SS*, as well as Goodrick-Clarke's two monographs, *Black Sun: Aryan Cults, Esoteric Nazism, and the Politics of Identity* and *The Occult Roots of Nazism*.

Nicholas Goodrick-Clarke, *The Occult Roots of Nazism: Secret Aryans Cults and Their Influence on Nazi Ideology*, (New York: Tauris Parke, 2005), 202.

Revolution's "conceivability" in *The Cultural Origins of the French Revolution*.[10] While works regarding the aforementioned academically preferred subjects, such as T.C.W. Blanning's *The Culture of Power and the Power of Culture*, offer insights the cultural paradigm shifts paving the way for the Revolution, historians need to begin spelunking the cultural historiography deeper than "the road to Revolutionary thought" and into the infamous period's radical religious culture.

Unfortunately, for now, there are barely any monographs specifically dedicated to the Cult of Reason and the Cult of the Supreme Being. Mona Ozouf's trailblazing study of the cults' fêtes, *Festivals and the French Revolution*, remains the titan of the historiography for the past twenty years. According to Ozouf, the state-mandated holidays granted legitimacy to the new Republic, marked the transformed nation as distinct from its *ancien régime* past, and indoctrinated the people with Revolutionary utopian propaganda.[11]

Although she highlights the Greco-Roman antique elements of the fêtes of the Cult of Reason and the Cult of the Supreme Being, the heart of Ozouf's research lies in the festivals' function as ceremonially reinforcing the social bonds among the French people in the midst of the Terror's chaos.[12] Ozouf argues that French policymakers and festival engineers desired to rid themselves of the old liturgical calendar for its inherent Catholicity, yet they understood the power of holidays to maintain social order and serve as an outlet for Dionysian impulses.[13] With the new festivals and cults, the French Republic avoided leaving a vacuum as dechristianization

---

[10] Roger Chartier, *The Cultural Origins of the French Revolution*, trans. Lydia G. Cochrane (Durham, North Carolina: Duke University Press, 1991) 2, 91.

[11] Mona Ozouf, *Festivals and the French Revolution*, trans. Alan Sheridan (Cambridge, Massachusetts: Harvard University Press, 1988), 11, 282.

[12] Ibid., 10-11.

[13] Ibid., 1-4, 9.

ripped away the rituals and emblems of the Gallican Church, while also promoting the utopian ideology of the Revolution.[14]

Through her study, Ozouf highlights the various ways in which the state cults emulated elements from Roman Catholicism, while also borrowing motifs from antiquity. She does not explore, however, the role of the Occult as an influence in the construction of France's idealistic, Neo-Classical religions.

Following Ozouf's research into the Republic's promotion of revolutionary ideals through culture, Lynn Hunt explores the cultural imagery and rhetoric crafted during the Revolution in *Politics, Culture, and Class in the French Revolution.* According to Hunt, this engineered political culture of the French Revolution molded and shaped France, thereby allowing unity and cohesion within this diverse society.[15] Hunt's research fixates upon the influence of symbols and rhetoric during revolutionary France, instead of just the religions or fêtes.

In Hunt's estimation, rhetoric and symbols created a national solidarity in the French people during the tumultuous era of the Revolution.[16] Through conspiratorial, anti-party rhetoric, figures such as Robespierre forged the people into a unified nation that glorified an idealized Greco-Roman brand of liberty.[17] The radical rhetoric, fearing the return of the Old Regime, stressed a sharp break with all past French customs, which in turn fueled the creation of new symbols to fill the cultural void.[18] This new culture did not reflect nationalism, but rather created

---

[14] Ibid., 268.

[15] Lynn Hunt, *Politics, Culture, and Class in the French Revolution* (Berkley: University of California Press, 1984), 14.

[16] Ibid., 24.

[17] Ibid., 28, 44, 46-7.

[18] Ibid., 50, 56, 88.

it: it unified people of different socio-economic statuses, both in the core and periphery.[19] By emphasizing rationalism, universalism, and communalism, Revolutionary cultural practices created national unity.[20] Hunt's research focuses upon symbols such as Marianne as a rallying point for all the French.[21] While she does discuss some of the Classical and masonic influences in Marianne's and the festivals' designs, Hunt does not analyze in-depth the religious-intellectual roots of Marianne's attributes or how the pre-Revolution cultural environment made the state's religious imagery possible.[22]

The revolutionary calendar has become a growing favorite regarding the analysis of revolutionary culture. Matthew Shaw's *Time and the French Revolution: The Republican Calendar, 1789-Year XIV* provides insights into calendar committee chairman Charles-Gilbert Romme's desire for decimal standardization in the new regime time keeping system.[23] While Shaw does acknowledge the role of nature goddess (e.g., Isis) and astrological imagery in the calendar's visual language, he pays it little heed beyond a brief mention as respectively symbolic of regeneration and the seasons.[24] Shaw's survey serves as a strong overview of the singular area of revolutionary timekeeping, but ignores the blatantly occult and pagan symbolism infused throughout *le calendrier republicain.*

French literary specialist Dan Edelstein is on the avant-garde of Enlightenment studies. Known for his evolving Internet database via Stanford University's digital library, *The Super-Enlightenment,* Edelstein's pet area of research is the role of unreason in the Age of Reason (e.g., the prevalence of "irrationality" during the Enlightenment, such as astronomer-cum-freemason

---

[19] Ibid., 123, 148, 167.

[20] Ibid., 123.

[21] Ibid., 219.

[22] Ibid., 60-61.

[23] Robert Shaw, *The Republican Calendar, 1789-Year XIV* (Rochester, New York: Boydell Press, 2011), 88.

[24] Ibid., 67-68, 71-72.

Jean-Sylvain Bailly's *Lettres sur l'Atlantide de Platon et sur l'ancienne histoire de l'Asie*, the

fruit of his obsession with locating Plato's lost civilization of Atlantis).[25] In his political and

intellectual history, *The Terror of Natural Right: Republicanism, the Cult of Nature, and the

French Revolution*, Edelstein's analysis of the influence of the millennia-old Golden Age myth,

as a driving force in the Terror's political philosophy, stands closest to the heart of this study's

exploration of the state cults.

Edelstein beautifully outlines the literary history of the Golden Age concept, from Hesiod

to the comte de Bougainville's descriptions of Tahiti as a prelapsarian society, as well as taking

note of important Golden Age motifs in political and literary history, such as the goddess of

justice, Astraea.[26] According to Edelstein, the Golden Age myth garnered many fans among the

philosophes, but many did not believe in it as an actual historical reality until early

anthropological studies, such as Voltaire's research on ancient India in *Essai sur les moeurs er

l'esprit des nations*.[27] These examinations into non-Western cultures supported the possibility of

a real Golden Age, because these more "natural" people groups (e.g., Gangarid Indians,

Tahitians, New World natives, etc.) lived closer to the ideal state than the French under the

Bourbons.[28] *Les bons sauvages* living in tribal "republics" (as Voltaire described the New World

natives' government), Enlightenment philosophers argued, mirrored the government during the

---

[25]Dan Edelstein, "About," *The Super-Enlightenment*,
http://collections.stanford.edu/supere/page.action?forward=about (accessed February 20, 2014).
Edelstein, "Jean-Sylvain Bailly (1736-1793)," *The Super-Enlightenment*,
http://collections.stanford.edu/supere/page.action?forward=author_jean_sylvain_bailly§ion=authors
(accessed February 20, 2014).
[26] Edelstein, *The Terror of Natural Right*, 10-13, 25.
[27] Ibid., 13, 90.
[28] Ibid., 93-99.

mythical Golden Age, thereby making this Eden-esque period no longer seem as fanciful and unrealistic as it once did.[29]

While Edelstein discusses the signature elements of the Greco-Roman Golden Age tale, such as Saturn and Astraea's presence as well as its related eschatology, he leashes these ideas to the stump of Enlightenment political philosophy and the Terror.[30] For Edelstein, dechristianized France under the rule of Nature meant a method for legitimizing the Terror's policies and laws.[31] Since law in the context of the Golden Age myth translated into the rule of Nature for the likes of Saint-Just and Robespierre, anyone who broke the law automatically became against Nature—unnatural—and therefore could no longer be a citizen of the French Natural state.[32] Such logic provides the rationale for denying people due process.[33] Because he centers upon the political ramifications of believing in the Golden Age, Edelstien leaves by the wayside how this belief explicitly related to the cults.

Adam Zamoyski in his survey of various revolutions' religiosity, *Holy Madness: Romantics, Patriots, and Revolutionaries, 1776-1871,* openly attempts to make no argument or analysis.[34] Spanning the ideological influence of American independence of the eighteenth century to the chain of Latin American revolutions in the nineteenth century, Zamoyksi traces the common strains of Romantic religious impulse as the new nations inherited a secularized form of divine right from the kings that they had deposed.[35]

---

[29] Ibid., 93, 118.

[30] Ibid., 189.

[31] Ibid., 4-5.

[32] Ibid., 14-15, 18, 21.

[33] Ibid., 18.

[34] Adam Zamoyski, *Holy Madness: Romantics, Patriots, and Revolutionaries, 1776-1871* (New York: Viking, 1999), xi.

[35] Ibid.

Zamoyski offers a unique approach to the cults of the French Revolution by putting them within a larger international context (or, arguably, an Atlantic one, since all of these events focus on three of the four Atlantic continents). In his discussion of the French Revolution's international influence, Zamoyski offers the interesting insight that France fancied itself as a neo-Roman Empire by strutting its hegemony everywhere it could.[36] For example, "in Switzerland, where France felt a God-given right to exert her influence," symbols of the new French secularized beliefs imposed themselves, such as the "tree of liberty crowned with a red bonnet…planted in every [Swiss] village."[37]

Unfortunately, though, Zamoyski's broad sweeping historical survey stunts his ability to craft fully developed insights into the French Revolution's state cults. He does make sharp insights, such as the Napoleon's establishment of himself as continental hegemon was "merely" a continuation of France's belief, during the Revolutionary Wars, that it was "the modern Rome" with the duty to impose its republican culture throughout Europe.[38] Another example of this weakness is in his discussion of the French republic "civil rites."[39] To Zamoyski, the Enlightenment's attempts at ridding itself of Christianity were fruitless because centuries of Christian-based culture and education had defined their very discourse. it was impossible.[40] "What they were peddling [instead] was a mongrel Christianity."[41] In analyzing the French cults' divinities, such as the goddess Liberty, Zamoyski sees a replacement for Jesus Christ or the Virgin Mary, instead of connecting the visual language and rhetoric surrounding Liberty with pre-Christian origins. This somewhat shallow approach to understanding the culture behind the

---

[36] Ibid., 110-112.
[37] Ibid., 111-112.
[38] Ibid., 110-111.
[39] Ibid., 65.
[40] Ibid., 3-4.
[41] Ibid., 4.

state deities is most likely a cause of Zamoyksi's extensive breadth of study. Discussions of Russia, Poland, Switzerland, Germany, Haiti, and more, however, drown out the sections that focus on French revolutionary mytho-religious views.

THIS STUDY'S PLACE WITHIN THE HISTORIOGRAPHY

Unfortunately, the French Revolution's historiography has yet to produce a study into how pre-Christian beliefs influenced the state cults. Too often, French Revolution historians treat the state cults like the world's most interesting footnote: a terrific anecdote to illustrate revolutionary radicalism, but little beyond that. It is the goal of this research to remedy this historiographic hole and try to understand what cultural factors made this eccentric episode in the Revolution possible. As such, this study shall take a three-pronged attack.

Chapter 1 analyzes the transference of Enlightenment Classicalism into the French Revolution. Enlightenment philosophers' fascination with the world of the ancient Greeks and Romans permeated their writings, which revolutionary readers such as Robespierre avidly studied. The idea that Classical civilization lived more rationally and naturally, and, therefore, ought to be emulated, influenced government leaders during the Terror to create new belief systems that would rebirth the pre-Christian traditions of antiquity. In this regard, much of the cults' creation, theology, and iconography stem from the *philosophes'* influence upon the French Revolution.

Chapter 2 answers the question of why would so much of the Catholic populace abandon their lifelong religious beliefs and participate in such paganized events as the *Fête* of Reason, which entailed the transforming of Notre Dame in Paris into the Temple of Reason. The French people's track record of Christian heterodoxy and fascination with magic and the Occult made the state cults easier to swallow for many in the population. Beginning in Louis XIV's France with the Affair of the Poisons to the French Occult underground's role in the development of Vodou in Saint-Domingue, Chapter 2 outlines that all things esoteric and fantastic intrigued the French—from Breton peasants to ladies at Versailles—long before the government mandated the religious remodeling. France already possessed a population practicing varying degrees of heresy; the jump from orthodoxy to apostasy may be wide, but such is not the case when moving from heresy to apostasy.

Chapter 3 discusses origins and roles of the foreign, antique imagery of Trojan hats, long-defunct goddesses in the cults. The appropriation of elements from long-defunct religions and heretical practices served as the Revolutionary leaders' way to boldly proclaim that the state's authority for republican government came from Nature herself—not the Judeo-Christian God, the Church, nor the monarchy. According to this subtle propaganda, the new Republic was the most natural and rational form of government, and, by following this government of Nature, France would lead the way in returning humanity to a long-lost Golden Age of rationality.[42] In this new Golden Age, the French would return to the traditions of their Classical forbears, because this original primitive religion was more "pure" and "natural."[43] Like the bizarre Nazi celebrations during the Third Reich, these cults masqueraded refurbished paganism as the new, official "rational" worldview for the French people. Also like the Nazis, the revolutionary leaders believed destiny appointed them the heralds of a new age: instead of a thousand-year Reich of Aryan supremacy, France would usher in a Saturnian era of equality for man.

Incidents such as the entire *fête* for the constitution—which showcased a giant, lactating sculpture of the Egyptian mother-goddess Isis—raises the question of how this nation of the

---

[42] Edelstein, *The Terror of Natural Right*, 181, 183-184, 186.

[43] Ozouf, *Festivals and the French Revolution*, 5.

Enlightenment evolved (or, rather, devolved) into a chaotic tyranny justifying itself through pre-Christian myth and belief. Placing these state religious spectacles in the light of France's history of heterodoxy, as well as the Republic's image of itself as the beckoner of Astraea, however, erodes some of the mystery behind the cults' festivals and imagery.

CHAPTER 1: THE INFILTRATION OF ENLIGHTENMENT CLASSICISM INTO THE FRENCH REVOLUTION

Although historians continue to debate as to the extent of the Enlightenment's influence upon the outbreak of the French Revolution, it is undeniable that the works of French *philosophes* shaped the ethos of the French Revolutionary leaders such as Maximilien Robespierre. Because Jean-Jacques Rousseau and the other *philosophes* served as inspirational figures for the Revolutionary leaders, an understanding of the *philosophes* and their own influences is imperative for an understanding of France's government during the infamous Reign of Terror. The influences upon the *philosophes* would in turn become influences upon the Revolutionary leaders. Due to the heavy influence of Classical Greco-Roman works in the philosophy of the Enlightenment, the writings of the *philosophes* operated as a conduit of Classical ideas into the French Revolution.

Some historians, such as Pierre Gaxotte, believe that the Enlightenment held little sway over the outbreak of the French Revolution, whereas others, such as Georges Lefebvre, see a direct connection between the salons of Paris and the storming of the Bastille.[1] Whether or not ideas or material matters (e.g., France's grain shortage around the time of the Revolution) were the stronger cause of the Revolution is not the primary concern of the following inquiry.[2] Even though the contest between material forces versus the impact of ideas in the Revolutionary

---

[1] Pierre Gaxotte, "The Enlightenment as Doctrinaire, Irreligious, and Conspiratorial," in *The Influence of the Enlightenment on the French Revolution*, ed. William F. Church, 2nd ed. (Lexington, Massachusetts: D.C. Heath and Company, 1974), 88.

Georges Lefebvre, "The *Declaration of the Rights of Man* as the Essence of the Enlightenment," in *The Influence of the Enlightenment on the French Revolution*, ed. William F. Church, 2nd ed. (Lexington, Massachusetts: D.C. Heath and Company, 1974), 123.

[2] William Doyle, *The Oxford History of the French Revolution*, 2nd ed. (New York: Oxford University Press Inc., 2002), 10, 20, 22, 86.

historiography rages on, what cannot be questioned is the influence of the Enlightenment after the outbreak of the Revolution.

A cursory glance at the historic literature of Revolutionary leaders reveals that important figures such as Robespierre, Roland Mirabeau, Louis-Antoine Léon de Saint-Just, and Sylvain Maréchal read Rousseau and other *philosophes'* writings avariciously.[3] Considering the vast levels of power these men held over the French people—such as possessing the power to rework the very nature of French religious culture and the role of the Church in one of the most Catholic countries of Europe—understanding the philosophies that influenced them enables the historian to better comprehend their motives and rationales during the fledgling French Republic's blood bath, the Terror.[4] To understand the intellectual undercurrents of the Revolutionary leaders is to understand the philosophical climate of the Revolution and Terror.

Although the Greek and Roman Classical influences upon French Enlightenment thinkers, such as Rousseau and Charles de Montesquieu, are dissected in the ensuing discussion below, these men were not wholly unique in their utilization of Classical sources.[5] Plutarch "was the most frequently read author [by men during the French Revolution] and that it was through him alone that men of the Revolution knew Greek antiquity."[6] The French's love of the Classical world went so far that even French chroniclers, such as the historian Fredegar appropriated the

---

[3] Charles Lyttle, "Deistic Piety in the Cults of the French Revolution," *Church History* Vol. 2, no. 1 (March 1933): 20.

[4] Ibid., 13.

Louis-Antoine Léon de Saint-Just, "13 November 1792 Speech," *Liberty, Equality, Fraternity: Exploring the French Revolution,* http://chnm.gmu.edu/revolution/d/320/ (accessed 1 November 2012).

John McManners, *The French Revolution and the Church* (New York: Harper Torchbooks, 1969), 86, 102-103.

[5] Peter Gay, *The Enlightenment: The Rise of Modern Paganism* (New York: W.W. Norton, 1966), 46-48, 68.

[6] Ozouf, *Festivals and the French Revolution,* 273.

genealogy of Homeric Troy as the origins of the Franks—a belief fostered through the Renaissance.[7]

What makes the *philosophes* and their influences from Classical civilization so noteworthy is the manner in which they acted as a filter of these Classical ideas to Robespierre and the other terrorists. Even the *philosophes'* motives for their fascination with the Mediterranean pagans shaped the template of thought for the terrorists and dechristianizers.[8] For much of the writings of the French Enlightenment was part of these intellectuals' struggle to rip Europe from its Christian heritage—in the name of reason and rationality, of course.[9]

To the French philosophers, studying the advanced civilizations of antiquity (e.g., Greece, Rome, China, India, etc.) was the perfect tool for aiding them in their goal to dismantle the authority of the Church, and thereby pry France from the arms of what they considered "superstition."[10] In looking to the ancient past, Voltaire, for example, hoped to prove that Christianity was not the highpoint of civilization, because he believed that Christianity was an irrational belief system.[11] In his vast historical survey, *Essai sur les moeurs et l'esprit des nations*, Voltaire asserted that the Orient achieved greatness well before the rise of Christendom:

---

[7] Although it should be noted that claiming such fanciful origins was not unique to France. For example, Charlemagne called himself the heir of Rome and Troy. For further information see chapters two and three of Lewis M. Greenberg's *Let There Be Darkness: The Reign of the Swastika.*

Peter G. Bietenholz, *Historia and Fabula: Myths and Legends in Historical Thought from Antiquity to the Modern Age* (Leiden, The Netherlands: E. J. Brill, 1994), 190-192.

[8] Gay, *The Enlightenment: The Rise of Modern Pagan*, xi.

[9] Ibid.

[10] Ironically for the *philosophes*, the Church was not the sole perpetuator of "superstition" during the eighteenth-century, as expounded upon later in Chapter 2. Many in France held an interest in esotericism and folk magic rooted in pre-Christian traditions.
Ibid., 4, 8.

[11] Jyoti Mohan, "La civilization la plus antique: Voltaire's Images of India," *Journal of World History* 16, no. 2 (June 2005), 184.

> *Il eût été souhaiter qu'il n'eût pas oublie entièrement les anicens peuples de l'orient, comme les Indiens and les Chinois, qui ont été si considérables avant que les autres nation sussent formées....En vous instruisant en philosophie de ce qui concer ce globe, vouz portez d'abord votre vue sur l'orient, berceau de tous les arts, & qui a tout donné à l'occident.*[12]

The complex philosophical thought and political systems of the ancient non-Christians, such as the Greeks and Romans, in the philosophers' estimation, was superior to that of the Christian Middle Ages, because the culture of antiquity was more "natural."[13]

By "natural," Rousseau and the other *philosophes* meant that the more primitive cultures were "purer" and more rational than the societies that developed in the ensuing centuries. In accordance with Rousseau's beliefs regarding mankind, man is at his best when he is in his most natural state.[14] Christianity, in this worldview, fell under the umbrella of an "irrational" institution since it was not part of the cultural landscape of the early pagans. If the Church were removed from France, various *philosophes* (and, in turn, major Revolutionary figures) believed, then the Golden Age[15] written of in antiquity by the likes of Hesiod and Virgil would return.[16] To the French intellectuals, such as Denis Diderot, the concept of a Classical Golden Age was not

---

[12] Loosely translated: "It is the hope [of this study] to not forget the ancient peoples of the Orient, like the Indians and the Chinese, who had been so great before any nations formed....In the learning the philosophy of the known world, first look to the East, the cradle of all arts, and who has given everything to the West."

Voltaire, *Œuvres complètes de Voltaire: Essair sur le mœurs et l'esprit des nations,* ed. Antoine-Augustin Renouard (Paris: 1819), 1:227, Google Books, http://books.google.com/books?id=LZ0MAQAAMAAJ&printsec=frontcover&source=gbs_ge_summary_r&cad=0#v=onepage&q&f=false (accessed March 9, 2014).

[13] Gordon H. McNeil, "The Cult of Rousseau and the French Revolution," *Journal of the History of Ideas* Vol. 6, no. 2 (April 1945): 211.

Emmet Kennedy, *A Cultural History of the French Revolution* (New Haven: Yale University Press, 1989), 61.

[14] Jean-Jacques Rousseau, "A Discourse on a Subject Proposed by the Academy of Dijon: What is the Origin of the Inequality Among Men, and Is It Authorised by Natural Law?" trans. G. D. H. Cole, http://www.constitution.org/jjr/ineq.htm (accessed 10 October 2012).

[15] More on the Golden Age shall be explored in Chapter 3.

[16] Gay, *The Enlightenment,* 125.

Edelstein, *The Terror of Natural Right,* 6, 12-13, 50-51, 53, 75.

mere mythology, but fact.[17] This belief in a return to man's more natural state (which Voltaire believed was Classical republicanism) fueled and shaped the policies of the French Revolutionary government.[18] In turn, Robespierre was bitten by the mania for a French Golden Age, as discussed in detail in Chapter 3.[19]

ROUSSEAU: THE FAVORITE OF ROBESPIERRE

In analyzing Robespierre's intellectual influences that sparked his French police state and even his more bizarre religious agendas, almost all trails lead back to Jean-Jacques Rousseau.[20] For example, when analyzing the authoritarian government of the Revolution, the Rousseauist fascination with the Spartan Lycurgus becomes apparent.[21] According to Plutarch—whom almost all French men read as youths—Lycurgus established the Spartan senate, thereby creating a balance of powers in the Spartan government.[22] In Rousseau's references to the half-mythical Lycurgus, it is evident that he believed that the somewhat dictatorial Spartan law-giver embodied early man's ideal in contrast to "modern corruption."[23] Rousseau's fascination and praise of Lycurgus and its transference to Robespierre becomes apparent when drawing direct comparisons between Robespierre and Lycurgus.[24] For example, operating in an intellectual vein along similar lines as Rousseau's belief that man ought to be as free as possible from "civilizing"

---

[17] Ibid., 13.

[18] Ibid., 93.

[19] Ibid., 23-24.

[20] Lyttle, "Deistic Piety in the Cults of the French Revolution," 20.

[21] Jean-Jacques Rousseau, *The Social Contract* (Adelaide, Australia: University of Adelaide, 2012), http://ebooks.adelaide.edu.au/r/rousseau/jean_jacques/r864s/index.html

(accessed 30 October 2012).

[22] Plutarch, *Lives,* ed. Arthur Hugh Clough, trans. John Dryden (New York: The Modern Library, 2001), 1:57.

[23] Plutarch, *Lives,* 60-61, 64, 76.

Judith N. Shklar, "Rousseau's Two Models: Sparta and the Age of Gold," *Political Science Quarterly* 18, no. 1 (March 1996): 31-32, 35-35, 44-45.

[24] Edelstein, *The Terror of Natural Right,* 82-83.

forces, Lycurgus did not allow his laws to be written down.[25] In doing so, Lycurgus argued that the Spartan legal code would serve the state better as being written in the heart of each citizen.[26] Considering the chaotic nature of the Revolutionary government with its lack of a properly written legal code—citing that nature is the highest authority and the embodiment of Revolutionary law itself—it is interesting to see the similarities between Lycurgus and the terrorist government.[27]

Rousseau's interpretations of Lycurgus' reign also manifest in the *philosophe*'s fascination with Spartan military virtue.[28] In Rousseau's estimation, military virtue was the perfect example of citizen virtue.[29] Given his fixation upon the concept of community and his ill-defined "general will" of the people, it is not surprising that the sentimental Rousseau would admire militarism in a society such as Sparta.[30] According to Plutarch's biography of Lycurgus, the Spartan lawgiver, too, shared the belief that a good citizen is a good soldier.[31] Such sentiments can be heard echoing in revolutionary France's full mobilization of the state—the *levée en masse*—which the Republic's leaders enacted as a clarion call of all Frenchmen to join as a national unit and fight for liberty.[32]

Classical influence in Rousseau is also apparent from his own claims about his intellectual influences. According to his own testimony, Rousseau spent his formative years

---

[25] Rousseau, "A Discourse on a Subject Proposed by the Academy of Dijon: What is the Origin of the Inequality Among Men, and Is It Authorised by Natural Law?"
Plutarch, *Lives*, 63.
[26] Ibid.
[27] Edelstein, *The Terror of Natural Right*, 2-4, 17.
Plutarch, *Lives*, 63.
Lynn Hunt, *Politics, Culture, and Class in the French Revolution*, 47.
[28] Shklar, "Rousseau's Two Models," 33.
[29] Ibid., 34-5.
[30] Ibid., 34-6.
[31] Plutarch, *Lives*, 66-68, 74.
[32] Doyle, *The Oxford History of the French Revolution*, 204.

devouring Plutarch's biographies of nigh-legendary Greeks and Romans.[33] The development of his love of men such as Cato and Brutus during his formative years makes the Classical world a prime factor in the shaping of Rousseau's Romantic worldview. Although his descriptions of ancient Sparta and Rome reveal a high level of idealization (e.g., his description of the Peloponnesian city-state belongs more in the realm of fantasy than of history: most of it was based upon his imagination), the factualness of Rousseau's knowledge of Classical civilization is not the main issue.[34] What matters is that Classical influences (whether accurate or not) are present in Rousseau's writing and philosophy, because his works shaped the fate of France during the tumultuous years of the Revolution.

Although Rousseau was long dead by the time the Jacobins took over France, he maintained a strong presence in the heart of French intellectualism. As the Great Terror sped closer and closer to its bloody climax with the death of Robespierre himself, Rousseau maintained a tangible presence in French philosophy. As head of the terrorist government, Robespierre—an avid Rousseauist—used his power and influence to create and implement his own state cult dedicated to the worship of Nature and Reason.[35] Part of this cult entailed an apotheosis of Rousseau: the Swiss philosopher in the new anti-Christian French religion became deified for his philosophical contributions.[36] This pantheonization of Rousseau by the republican government leaves no doubt that Rousseau made an impact upon the thinking of revolutionary leaders.[37] Although tracing the diffusion of ideas from one historical figure to another is a rather

---

[33] Shklar, "Rousseau's Two Models," 32.

Gay, *The Enlightenment*, 46.

Jean-Jacques Rousseau, *The Confessions of Jean-Jacques Rousseau*, ed. David Widger, http://www.gutenberg.org/files/3913/3913-h/3913-h.htm (accessed 20 October 2012).

[34] Shklar, "Rousseau's Two Models," 32.

[35] McNeil, "The Cult of Rousseau and the French Revolution," 208.

[36] Ibid.

[37] Ibid., 208, 211-212.

fluid process—too often based more upon speculation rather than hard evidence—the blatant state-mandated worship of Rousseau leaves little room to question whether or not Rousseau was an influential force in the policies of the French Republic.[38]

With his pessimistic views of the future of humanity, Rousseau preferred instead to find models for society in an idealized image of Greco-Roman civilization.[39] As with his lauding of dictatorial republics such as Sparta (instead of the exclusive democracy of Athens), Rousseau praised more authoritarian forms of government to help a nation's citizenry achieve "freedom."[40] Considering his fixation upon naturalness and the idea that civilization was a corrupting force, it is interesting that Rousseau would favor such heavy control of people's lives by their nation.[41] Rousseau, however, is notorious in literary history for his ambiguous and ever-contradicting views.[42]

Ambiguous or not, what makes Rousseau's ideas, concerning what he deemed the ideal government for the rebirth of his Greco-Roman Golden Age, so dangerous is the fact that Robespierre swallowed these ideas whole.[43] As historians Lester G. Crocker and Henri Peyre point out, Robespierre's radical ideas regarding the reshaping of France into a Classically influenced Republic under the aegis of Nature stem from Rousseau's writings.[44] This attempt to recreate a mythical Golden Age from ancient times by Robespierre and the revolutionaries

---

[38] McNeil, "The Cult of Rousseau and the French Revolution," 208.
Kennedy, *A Cultural History of the French Revolution*, 155, 331.
[39] Lester G. Crocker, "Rousseau's General Will and Revolutionary Dictatorship," in *The Influence of the Enlightenment on the French Revolution*, ed. William F. Church, 2nd ed., (Lexington, Massachusetts: D.C. Heath and Company, 1974), 151.
[40] Ibid., 157.
Shklar, "Rousseau's Two Models," 36.
[41] Ibid., 36, 48.
[42] Crocker, "Rousseau's General Will and Revolutionary Dictatorship,"150.
[43]Ibid., 156-157.
[44]Ibid.
Henri Peyre, "The Influence of Eighteenth-Century Ideas on the French Revolution," in *The Influence of the Enlightenment on the French Revolution*, ed. William F. Church, 2nd ed. (Lexington, Massachusetts: D.C. Heath and Company, 1974), 161, 169, 182.

eventually hailed policies such as the massive dechristianization program. By planting the seeds

for the revolutionaries' pursuit of an ideal nation ruled by Nature and promoting authoritarian

government, Rousseau's writings are responsible for the persecution of hundreds of thousands of

French Christians.[45] Whether Rousseau intended or would have favored such actions is not

important; the fact that he inspired the actions, however, is.

Because Rousseau's writings, such as *The Social Contract* and his *Discourses*, were such

powerful forces in the worldview of the Robespierre and his Jacobin fellow-travelers, it is only

logical that Rousseau's influences would manifest in the Jacobin government. Since Rousseau's

work possessed such an admiration of and influence from the Greco-Roman world, these factors

in Rousseau's writings would pass into the worldview of the terrorists.

VOLTAIRE: ANTIQUITY AS AN ALTERNATIVE TO CHRISTIANITY

Another pantheonized giant from the Enlightenment is Voltaire.[46] Although he disagreed

with Rousseau's fascination with primitivism (i.e., the idea that man in a more natural state of

being, apart from the corrupting influences of society, is the ideal way of being), Voltaire did,

however, share with the Swiss philosopher an interest in Classical antiquity.[47]

Whereas Rousseau's writings vary with his point of view depending at which point in his

life he penned the work in question, Voltaire maintained a clear, sharp, consistent perspective as

---

[45] McManners, *The French Revolution and the Church*, 88.

[46] Ibid., 98.

[47] Ozouf, *Festivals and the French Revolution*, 5.

Rousseau, "A Discourse on a Subject Proposed by the Academy of Dijon: What is the Origin of the Inequality Among Men, and Is It Authorised by Natural Law?"

Gay, *The Enlightenment*, 5.

Mohan, "La civilization la plus antique," 175, 181, 184.

a philosopher.[48] A militant critic of the Church and religion in general, Voltaire dove into ancient

Mediterranean history as means of undermining the authority of the Church.[49]

Reading works by Classical authors such as Strabo and Pliny, Voltaire searched ancient

history in the hopes of finding evidence of intellectual roots pre-dating the rise of Christianity.[50]

In his research, he came to the conclusion (as he states at the beginning of his *Siècle de Louis

XIV*) that two of the happiest ages of man were in Periclean Athens and Ciceronian Rome.[51] In

his view (which was shared by the other *philosophes*, such as Rousseau and Diderot), the

Christian-dominated Middle Ages were, in comparison to antiquity, backward and a period of

darkness.[52] In Voltaire's estimation, the ancients were more tolerant and less superstitious than

the Christians of Scholastic Europe.[53] By highlighting the intellectual achievements and the

advanced (i.e., "tolerant") mindsets of the ancient Greeks and Romans, Voltaire aimed to

undermine the idea that Christian Europe was the greatest civilization.[54] In doing so, he hoped to

free Europeans' minds from the supposed shackles of Christian intellectual influence (which he

dubbed as superstitious) and, instead, move toward secularism.[55]

Voltaire and his campaign to undermine Christianity and put Greco-Roman practices

upon a pedestal caused him to do mental gymnastics. At one point, he labels the Orphic

Mysteries as rationalistic—as a sort of proto-monotheistic cult that was kept shrouded in secret

---

[48] Crocker, "Rousseau's General Will and Revolutionary Dictatorship," 150.
Peyre, "The Influence of Eighteenth-Century Ideas on the French Revolution," 180.
[49] Mohan, "La civilization la plus antique," 184.
Gay, *The Enlightenment*, 8.
[50] Mohan, "La civilization la plus antique," 175, 184
[51] Gay, *The Enlightenment*, 35.
Voltaire, *Age of Louis XIV*, ed. Tobias Smollett, trans. William F. Fleming (New York: E.R. DuMont, 1901), http://oll.libertyfund.org/index.php?option=com_staticxt&staticfile=show.php%3Ftitle=2132&layout=html (accessed 12 November 2012).
[52] Gay, *The Enlightenment*, 35-6.
[53] Ibid., 51.
[54] Ibid., 51, 71.
[55] Ibid.

to prevent rousing the anger of the great unwashed.[56] Considering that the Orphic Mysteries were fertility and agricultural rites performed by frenzied, ecstatic women in honor of a mythical figure whose music was fabled to cause the crops to grow, this is quite a mental leap on Voltaire's part.[57] To put it mildly, there is nothing rationalistic or monotheistic about the Greek mystery religions. Voltaire came up with this unfounded theory because he could not come to terms with the idea that the ancient Greeks—the same culture that produced great thinkers such as Plato, Aristotle, and Thales—possessed their own religious superstitions, which were possibly on par with (or worse than) the ones that Voltaire identified in his own time.[58]

This idea that the pagan rituals of the ancient Greeks—such as the Orphic and Eleusinian mysteries—were rationalistic, instead of superstitious, permeated from Voltaire's writings and the state cults of dechristianized France. For example, the revolutionary leaders lauded the cult ritual in dechristianized Notre Dame as a "triumph of reason over superstition."[59] These supposedly rationalistic cults, dedicated to reason and Nature, entailed women dressed as proxies of the Goddess of Liberty (Marianne) and also village worship magically-endowed liberty trees, (to just name a few pagan-derived elements).[60] Like Voltaire, Robespierre, David, and others who had a hand in the crafting of these secular religions of nature, the Terrorists believed that

---

[56] Ibid., 83.

[57] Martin P. Nilsson, *Greek Popular Religion*, (New York: Columbia University Press, 1940), 36, 42.

Jocelyn Godwin, "The Orphic Mysteries," *Rosicrucian Digest* no. 1 (2008): 48-49.

Charles Freeman, *The Greek Achievement: The Foundation of the Western World* (New York: Penguin Books, 1999), 141-142.

[58] Gay, *The Enlightenment*, 78-79, 83.

[59] Lyttle, "Deistic Piety in the Cults of the French Revolution," 25.

[60] Hunt, *Politics, Culture, and Class in the French Revolution*, 62.

Ozouf, *Festivals and the French Revolution*, 97-99, 101-102.

Plutarch, *Isis and Osiris*, trans. Frank Cole Babbitt, (Loeb Classical Library, 1978), 86-88, 101.

such ancient pagan elements were in fact more rational than the Christianity of the *ancien régime*.[61]

Although much of the dogmas of naturalism and primitivism in the Cult of Reason and the Cult of the Supreme Being are the intellectual progeny of Rousseau's *bon savage* beliefs, the pagan rituals of the cults themselves are indebted to Voltaire.[62] His anti-Christian agenda in the Enlightenment, which fuelled his quest to study Greco-Roman religious and intellectual history, directly influenced the dechristianization and rational-superstitious cults of Revolutionary France.[63]

Voltaire's writing helped inspire the most bizarre period of the Revolution. Through Voltaire's venomous anti-Christian bias and influence, the cross became a banned symbol; French citizens desacralized holy relics and had bacchanalia in town churches.[64] Attempting to undermine the Church's authority, Voltaire went so far as to call the ancient mystery religions rationalistic.[65] Given what little is known about these practices—they were dubbed mysteries for a reason—it is interesting the level of personal bias Voltaire succumbed to in his historical analysis of the Classical world.[66] As seen in the doctrine and propaganda of Robespierre's deistic cult, the French Revolution's religious program recycled openly from the Greco-Roman traditions, citing these practices as more rational in comparison to Christianity.[67]

---

[61] Ozouf, *Festivals and the French Revolution*, 274, 281.

[62] Rousseau, "A Discourse on a Subject Proposed by the Academy of Dijon: What is the Origin of the Inequality Among Men, and Is It Authorised by Natural Law?"

[63] Mohan, "La civilization la plus antique," 183-184.
Gay, *The Enlightenment*, xi, 35, 39, 51, 72.

[64] Ozouf, *Festivals and the French Revolution*, 145, 225.
McManners, *The French Revolution and the Church*, 93-94.

[65] Gay, *The Enlightenment*, 83.

[66] Freeman, *The Greek Achievement*, 141.

[67] Ozouf, *Festivals and the French Revolution*, 52.

Because Voltaire was deified in a pantheonization ritual during the Reign of Terror, it is without a doubt that the revolutionary leaders were familiar with his corpus of philosophical (and anti-Christian) work.[68] Thus, through Voltaire's biased historical research to assert his theory of Classical supremacy over Christian Scholasticism, Classical elements diffused from the Enlightenment and directly into the policies of the policies of the Reign of Terror's government.[69]

MONTESQUIEU'S INFLUENCE AS A HISTORIAN OF ROMAN SOCIETY

Although he was not given exact demigod-status in the new French government, Charles de Montesquieu was, nonetheless, "the most influential" early Enlightenment philosopher.[70] Famous for his biting commentary of contemporary Parisian society in his satire, *The Persian Letters*, Montesquieu later gained notoriety in France for his *The Spirit of the Laws*, which reshaped modern political theory and made him a major influence upon American revolutionary figures such as James Madison.[71] Montesquieu's philosophy shaped both political discussion in the Enlightenment and, later, the revolutionary governments in America and France.[72] His importance in France was so much so that his image was placed on the altar of Reason during the Fête of Reason.[73] As such a major intellectual figure in the Enlightenment and eventually government in the modern era, the Classical influences that permeated his influential writings merit analysis in their relation to the French Revolution.

---

[68] Kennedy, *A Cultural History of the French Revolution*, 331.

[69] Gay, *The Enlightenment*, 82-83.

[70] Owen Connelly, *The French Revolution and Napoleonic Era*, 3rd ed. (Boston: Wadsworth Cengage, 2000), 16.

[71] Susan Gordon, *Montesquieu: The French Philosopher Who Shaped Modern Government* (New York: Rosen Publishing Group, 2006), 79.

[72] Gordon, *Montesquieu: The French Philosopher Who Shaped Modern Government*, 78.

[73] Lyttle, "Deistic Piety in the Cults of the French Revolution," 24.

One obvious indicator that Montesquieu's work contained Greco-Roman influences is the fact that he composed an entire history of Rome.[74] Predating Gibbon's monumental tome detailing the fall of the Roman Empire, Montesquieu's historical inquiry focuses on what made Rome great and what set in motion its downfall.[75] In his *Considerations on the Causes of Greatness of the Romans and their Decline*, Montesquieu eloquently champions early Rome, citing Rome along with Sparta as two of history's most powerful republics.[76] According to Montesquieu's historical perspective, the early Republic of Rome was blessed with a line of benevolent rulers.[77] Montesquieu argued that ancient Rome illustrates the principle that the ruler of a nation is the first citizen of the state, and, therefore, is especially accountable unto the laws and the people.[78] These sentiments are echoed in Saint-Just's speech calling for the prosecution of Louis XVI:

> I shall undertake, citizens, to prove that the King can be judged. . . . I say that the King should be judged as an enemy and that even more than judge him, we must fight him....Perhaps one day, men as far removed from our prejudices as we are from those of the Vandals will be astonished by the barbarity of an age in which the judging of a tyrant was thought to be something sacred.... One day men will be astonished by the fact that humanity in the eighteenth century was less advanced than in the time of Caesar. Then a tyrant was slain in the midst of the Senate with no formalities but thirty blows of a dagger and with no other law save the liberty of Rome.[79]

---

[74] Charles de Montesquieu, *Considerations on the Causes of the Greatness of the Romans and their Decline*, trans. David Lowenthal (New York: The Free Press, 1734), http://www.constitution.org/cm/ccgrd_l.htm (accessed 30 October 2012).

[75] Montesquieu, *Considerations on the Causes of the Greatness of the Romans and their Decline*.

[76] Ibid.

[77] Ibid.

Catherine Volpilhac-Auger, "*Considérations sur les causes de la grandeur des Romains et de leur décandence*," *Dictionnaire électronique Montesquieu*, http://dictionnaire-montesquieu.ens-lyon.fr/index.php?id=196 (accessed 10 November 2012).

[78] Montesquieu, *Considerations on the Causes of the Greatness of the Romans and their Decline*.

[79] Louis-Antoine Léon de Saint-Just, "13 November 1792 Speech."

Another element of Montesquieu's history of Rome worthy of note is his mentioning that the early Roman Republic was able to maintain itself so well because every citizen served as soldier.[80] As with Rousseau's praise of Lycurgan Sparta's militarism, Montesquieu's praise of a Classical republic's militarism and full mobilization through citizen-soldiery is reflected in the implementation of the *levée en masse*.[81] The concepts behind revolutionary France's clarion call for all citizens to take up arms in the name of *la patrie* are better encapsulated in the original language than in the English translation. *Levée en masse* in the original French held the connotations that the citizen-soldiers were to rise up for any reason without goading by or specific instructions from the state.[82] The original concept, therefore, entails more than a massive conscription for war. [83] In this mode of thought, citizens are much more autonomous in their roles as soldiers, as was the ideal in early Rome.[84] Citizenship and soldiery were one and the same in Rome, hence the fact that Rome never fully experienced demobilization.[85] This Classical citizen-soldier ideal is inherent in the *levée en masse*.[86] Thus, considering Montesquieu served as the premiere French political philosopher of the Enlightenment, and his works are noted for their influence in the birthing of modern government, his praise of Classical citizen-soldiery possesses likely connections to revolutionary France's *lévee en masse*.

---

[80]Montesquieu, *Considerations on the Causes of the Greatness of the Romans and their Decline*, 162.

[81] Doyle, *The Oxford History of the French Revolution*, 204, 340.

[82] R. Claire Snyder, *Citizen-Soldiers and Manly Warriors: Military Service and Gender in the Civic Republican Tradition*, (Lanham, Maryland: Rowman & Littlefield Publishers, 1999), 68.

[83] Ibid.

[84] Ibid.

Claude Nicolet, *The World of the Citizen in Republican Rome*, trans. P.S. Falla (Berkley: University of California Press, 1980), 8.

[85] Ibid., 92.

[86] Snyder, *Citizen-Soldiers and Manly Warriors*, 69.

Perhaps the most important element of Baron de Montesquieu's historical research is his argument that the Romans appealed to natural, universal law.[87] After reading the commentaries of Romans such as Polybius and Cicero, Montesquieu came to the conclusion that the Roman view of slavery stemmed from the concept that there is universal law of man as mandated by nature.[88] This was in contrast, according to Montesquieu, to Platonic and Aristotelian arguments that slavery was the natural state of all non-Greeks.[89] The Romans, instead, believed that all men in their natural state were free and that slavery was an institution created by society.[90]

This argument that Roman philosophy espoused the view that man's natural state (and, therefore, in Rousseauist philosophy, man's ideal state) manifests itself in the cries of *"liberté, egalité, et fraternité."* In revolutionary France's cult fête in honor of the republican constitution, this idea that freedom is the gift of Nature mirrors Montesquieu's own analysis of the Romans.[91] Thus, since Montesquieu did achieve venerable celebrity status in the revolutionary cults, traces of his Classically influenced ideas and works manifest in the culture and policies implemented by the government leaders.[92]

MONTESQUIEU'S INLFUENCE AS A POLITICAL THEORIST

Besides writing history, Montesquieu's most distinct literary mark hails from his work as a political theorist. Montesquieu's magnum opus, *The Spirit of the Laws*, possesses elements from Greco-Roman civilization, which in turn offers influence on the government of the French Revolution.

---

[87] Montesquieu, *Considerations on the Causes of the Greatness of the Romans and their Decline,* 415.

[88] Ibid.

[89] Ibid., 170-180, 415.

[90] Ibid., 415.

[91] Edelstein, *The Terror of Natural Right,* 180-181.

[92] Lyttle, "Deistic Piety in the Cults of the French Revolution," 24.

Although most of his *The Spirit of the Laws* operates as an analysis of different forms of government and his perspective that a three-pronged government of checks and balances makes for the best and most effective state, he does, however make many allusions to Greco-Roman society and government.[93]

Of particular note in Book VI of *The Spirit of the Laws* is Montesquieu's reference that the ancient Romans were free to accuse each other of not being a good citizen, and that this was "agreeable to the spirit of a republic, where each citizen ought to have an unlimited zeal for the public good, and is supposed to hold all the rights of his country in his own hands."[94] This statement echoes several sentiments floating around in the intellectual atmosphere both before and during the French Revolution. For one, this mirrors Rousseau's statements regarding the importance of the common good.[95] A more eerie comparison, however, can be drawn between the ideas of Roman citizens lawfully accusing one another and French citizens denouncing each other during the Reign of Terror.[96]

Although this comparison is more based upon inference than a hard piece of evidence from a revolutionary leader's own words, and, therefore, could be merely a coincidence, it is a point still worth considering. After all, Montesquieu was the most influential philosopher of the Enlightenment in general and his *Spirit of the Laws* is an iconic work of the period.[97] It is

---

[93] Charles de Montesquieu, *The Spirit of the Laws*, http://www.constitution.org/cm/sol-02.htm (accessed 2 November 2012).

[94] Ibid.

[95] Rousseau, *The Social Contract.*

[96] Montesquieu, *The Spirit of the Laws.*

Simon Schama, *Citizens: A Chronicle of the French Revolution* (New York: Alfred A. Knopf, 1989), 434-435.

David Andress, *The Terror: The Merciless War for Freedom in Revolutionary France* (New York: Farrar, Straus and Giroux, 2006), 167, 345-37.

[97] Connelly, *The French Revolution and Napoleonic Era,* 16.

therefore unlikely that the similarities between his statements and the events of the Reign of Terror are solely the working of mere chance.

As with Rousseau, Montesquieu reveals himself as a fan of Lycurgan Sparta as well as early Rome.[98] The multiple references French *philosophes* make to Plutarch's biography of Lycurgus cannot help but raise the question of whether or not Revolutionary France was an attempt at creating a Lycurgan France—that is, a Classical, authoritarian republic with a fully mobilized citizenry operating under natural law. At this stage in the historiography of the French Revolution, however, it is difficult to gauge if this was truly the case. For now, such thoughts are more suited to the realm of speculation than historical fact.

DAVID: THE ENLIGHTENMENT'S FASCINATION WITH CLASSICISM IN PICTURES

Although the heralded figures from the Enlightenment were dead by the time of the French Revolution, Neo-Classical painter Jacques-Louis David began his artistic career in the years before the Revolution. His career—which spanned the years preceding the Revolution, to his role as the artistic director of revolutionary France, and finally as the court painter of Napoleon Bonaparte—offers insights into the carry-over of the Classical influences of the Enlightenment (in this case via aesthetic forms) into the policies of France during the Jacobins' governance.[99]

Classicism is the key theme in all of David's work, and it owes its strong presence to his artistic training in Rome.[100] The discovery of the ruins of Pompeii and Herculaneum spawned a

---

[98] Montesquieu, *The Spirit of the Laws.*

[99] Carol Strickland, *The Annotated Mona Lisa* (Kansas City: Andrews and McMeel, 1992), 69.

[100] David Lloyd Dowd, *Pageant-Master of the Revolution: Jacques-Louis David and the French Revolution* (Freeport, New York: Books for Libraries Press, 1948), 4.

revitalized interest during the Enlightenment in Classical aesthetics.[101] This renewed interest inspired the young David to train in the Classical style in Rome.[102] During this period, he developed his signature technique of blending popular Neo-Classical content and themes with "morality and philosophy."[103]

As the face of Neo-Classicism in art history, David's early career acts as a visual bridge between the Classically influenced philosophies of the Enlightenment and the policies of the French revolutionary government.[104] Painted several years before the storming of the Bastille, David's stoic *Oath of the Horatii* served as a visual depiction of the Enlightenment's *zeitgeist* of reason, rationalism, and fascination with Greco-Roman themes.[105] This work placed him on the cultural map as presenting Enlightenment principles in the "clearest expression [of the]…neoclassicism of the eighteenth-century."[106]

Although this painting was a royally commissioned product of the Enlightenment, revolutionary leaders later adopted the painting for themselves and claimed it as an example of revolutionary ideology and values.[107] *Oath of the Horatii* stoically depicts a scene from Livy's historical writing and expresses the Enlightenment's "faith in reason and the rights of man."[108] Through the statuesque composition of the sons of Horatio, swearing their blood oaths to defend their family honor and Rome, David idealizes the *Romanitas* (i.e., the idealized "Roman-ness,"

---

[101] Ibid., 4-5.

[102] Ibid., 5.

[103] Ibid.

[104] Ibid.

Maiken Umbach, "Classicism, Enlightenment and the 'Other': thoughts on decoding eighteenth-century visual culture," *Art History*, no. 3 (June 2002): 325.

[105] "Neo-Classicism & the French Revolution," *Oxford Art Online,* http://www.oxfordartonline.com/public/page/themes/neoclassicismandthefrenchrevolution (accessed 14 November 2012).

[106] Umbach, "Classicism, Enlightenment and the 'Other'," 333.

[107] Hugh Honour, *Neo-Classicism* (New York: Penguin Books, 1977), 71.

[108] Ibid., 75.

encapsulating the ethos and behavior of every Roman citizen-soldier) of the Horatii.[109] When the contemporary artist Pierre-Paul Prud'hon later commented on the painting, the context of the *Oath of the Horatii* changed from a historical painting in the Classical style to a "manifesto of the Revolution."[110] In the minds of the revolutionaries, the royally commissioned painting depicted archetypal virtuous Romans swearing their lives to *la patrie* (i.e., the French fatherland—this word in French carries a more spiritual context, which is lost in translation to English).[111] With the way the revolutionaries interpreted the painting, it might as well have been commissioned by a leader such as Robespierre.[112]

The Oath of the Horatii became a perfect image for Revolutionary propaganda. Its visual embodiment of Republican virtue symbolized the ideals of the Jacobins: a state run by virtue.[113] The trickle of its Classical imagery from Livy's history from the Enlightenment into the spirit of the Revolution is evident in the anonymously composed print of the Tennis Court Oath.[114] The compositional details of the Horatii's arms, outstretched in a blood oath, are mirrored by the Third Estate in this print.[115] Thus, although there continues a lively debate within the art history community as to what David's political motives (if any) were behind this Neo-Classical masterwork, the fact remains that his art became part of the symbolic rhetoric of the

---

[109] Strickland, *The Annotated Mona Lisa*, 69.

"The Oath of the Horatii," *Louvre Museum*, http://www.louvre.fr/en/oeuvre-notices/oath-horatii (accessed 11 November 2012).

Andrew Merrills and Richard Miles, *The Vandals*, (London: Wiley-Blackwell, 2010), 88.

[110] Honour, *Neoclassicism*, 71-72.

[111] Ibid.

[112] Ibid.

[113] Dowd, *Pageant-Master of the Republic*, 120.

[114] Simon Schama, *Citizens: A Chronicle of the French Revolution* (New York: Alfred A. Knopf, 1989), 360.

[115] Ibid., 359-360.

Revolution.[116] This painting reflects David's interest in the burgeoning field of Classical archaeology and its subsequent impact upon the visual language of revolutionary France.[117]

A much more direct impact of David and his Classical influences manifested in his political career. Unlike the other members of the Enlightenment discussed in this inquiry into the Classical influences of the Enlightenment and their role in the Revolution, David actively participated in the commandeering of his works into the revolutionary government. In 1790, the Jacobins hired David as their artist in residence.[118] As an official member of the Jacobin club (and a close friend of Robespierre himself), David helped foster the Revolution's "cult of antiquity," making neo-classicism the official style of the new Republic.[119]

Although many of David's notable paintings in the annals of art history are from the Napoleonic era (save, say, his *Death of Marat*), he served as revolutionary France's artistic director. As the Jacobins dechristianized France and replaced Christianity with the secular state cults, David aided in crafting the aesthetics of the new naturalistic religions.[120] For example, David designed the statues of the Nature goddesses for the Fête of Reason and the Supreme Being, which did not survive long past the Great Terror.[121]

David's participation in the state cults went further than behind-the-scenes pre-production: he even participated alongside Robespierre in the Fête of the Supreme Being.[122] David acted as the ceremony's torchbearer and passed the torch to Robespierre, who then "ignited a cardboard statue of Atheism."[123] Involvement in culturally and politically significant

---

116 Ibid., 172-174, 359-361.

117 Dowd, *Pageant-Master of the Revolution*, 4.

118 Honour, *Neoclassicism*, 75.

119 Ibid.

120 Edelstein, *The Terror of Natural Right*, 184.

121 Ibid.

122 Dowd, *Pageant-Master of the Republic*, 123.

123 Ibid.

events, such as the Fête of the Supreme Being, highlight the influential role David held in Revolutionary France. As someone important enough to be a co-creator of the Cult of the Supreme Being, David's artistic works and their Classical themes, therefore, merit analysis for this inquiry of Greco-Romanism filtering from the Enlightenment into the Revolution.

Although accounts survive of David's monumental plaster works for the various secular religious festivals and his Revolutionary Greco-Roman-style commemorative medals, the actual works themselves have not outlasted Robespierre's regime.[124] With that in mind, historians must trust the eyewitnesses' testimony regarding the mimicry of ancient art in these grand sculptures' form and style.[125] His famous painting, *The Death of Socrates*, however, rests safely today in New York's Metropolitan Museum of Art.[126]

Predating the outbreak of the Revolution by two years, *The Death of Socrates* stands as a testament of the influence of Classicism in the Enlightenment.[127] Like *The Oath of the Horatii*, this painting rips a scene straight out of Greco-Roman antiquity and depicts it for an eighteenth-century French audience. Such a detailed depiction of Socrates' death makes it clear that David had a familiarity with Plato's *Phaedo*, thereby further illustrating the role of Classicism in the Enlightenment.[128]

By analyzing some of David's noteworthy Neo-Classical paintings, the influence of the Classical world upon the Enlightenment becomes apparent. David's long, illustrious career

---

[124] Ibid., 136.
Walter Friedlander, *David to Delacroix*, trans. Robert Goldwater (New York: Schocken Books, 1970), 22.
[125] Edelstein, *The Terror of Natural Right*, 185.
[126] Dowd, *Pageant-Master of the Republic*, 137.
"The Death of Socrates," *The Metropolitan Museum of Art*, *http://www.metmuseum.org/Collections/search-the-collections/110000543* (accessed 14 November 2012).
[127] Ibid.
[128] Plato, *Phaedo*, trans. Benjamin Jowlett (London: Oxford University Press,1892), http://oll.libertyfund.org/?option=com_staticxt&staticfile=show.php%3Ftitle=766&chapter=93700&layout=html&Itemid=27 (accessed 19 November 2012).

makes it clear that Classical influences played a major role in both the Enlightenment and the ensuing era. The epoch's fascination with Greco-Roman antiquity spawned an entire aesthetic movement—Neo-Classicism.[129] David's unique professional situation amongst the figures discussed in this inquiry (i.e., he lived through the Enlightenment and survived the Revolution into the Napoleonic era) further highlights the impact of Enlightenment Classicism upon the Revolution.[130] As someone whose career predated the French Revolution's outbreak and also thrived during the new Republic, David's work acts as a literal illustration of the carryover of the Enlightenment's Classical influences into the French Revolution and beyond. Through paintings such as *Oath of the Horatii*, Neo-Classicism became the official artistic style of the Revolutionary government and eventually shaped the religious aesthetics of the state's secular cults.[131] David's influence in the Revolution is, therefore, without question. The outside influences upon his own work (i.e., the world of Classical antiquity), therefore, deserve notice, because these influences, through the conduit of David's art, shaped Revolutionary culture.

CONCLUSIONS: WHY DELVE INTO THE ENLIGHTENMENT'S INFLUENCES?

Through the analysis of major Enlightenment figures—such as the philosophes Jean-Jacques Rousseau, Voltaire, and Charles de Montesquieu, as well as Neo-Classical painter Jacques-Louis David—the importance of Classical civilization's influence in the Age of Reason is apparent. The influences of these men warrant inquiry, because their ideas shaped the policies and practices of the Revolutionary government during its short lifespan.

---

[129] Dowd, *Pageant-Master of the Enlightenment*, 4.

[130] Strickland, *The Annotated Mona Lisa*, 69.

[131] Honour, *Neo-Classicism*, 171.

McManners, *The French Revolution and the Church*, 98-99.

The Classically influenced ideas of thinkers such as Rousseau did not die with the *ancien régime*. Although the *philosophes* lived under the Old Regime, their ideas paved the way for the breakdown of this way of life in Europe. It may be difficult to quantify how much of an impact an idea can have—ideas are intangible, and because just two people espouse similar ideas does not necessarily mean one influenced the other. Thus, with that fact in mind, the exact degree the Enlightenment had upon the French Revolution's leaders and the Reign of Terror may never fully be known. That being said, however, although historians may not be able to objectively quantify the Enlightenment's intellectual impact, the impact remains apparent nonetheless.

The Enlightenment's Classical influences trickled into the Revolution, because the Enlightenment was entangled in the policies of the new Republic. For example, Robespierre was an avid reader of Rousseau.[132] He was such a big fan that Rousseau became officially deified during Robespierre's reign.[133] Facts such as these—although they cannot offer quantifiable evidence of intellectual influence—nonetheless, offer a clear illustration of the importance of the Enlightenment in the hearts and minds of the revolutionaries. Although the secular religious practices of the Terror seem irrational, there was a method to the madness: Rousseau was not chosen for pantheonization for no small reason. He was already a major figure in the revolutionaries' minds well before his state-mandated worship.[134]

Rousseau's deification is just one tangible example of the Enlightenment's impact manifesting itself within the French Revolution. Montesquieu also held sway over the policies of the Revolution. Although not as much a polarizing figure as Rousseau, Montesquieu's political

---

[132] Lyttle, "Deistic Piety in the Cults of the French Revolution," 27.
McNeil, "The Cult of Rousseau and the French Revolution," 201-202.
[133] Ibid., 208.
Kennedy, *A Cultural History of the French Revolution,* 155, 331.
[134] McNeil, "The Cult of Rousseau and the French Revolution," 197.

philosophy gained a following on both sides of the Atlantic.[135] A fan of Sparta, like Rousseau, Montesquieu's influence during the Revolution was not only during the early days of the Revolution, when leaders such as the Comte de Mirabeau still aimed for a form of balanced, constitutional monarchy.[136] Montesquieu's love of *Romanitas* and the Greco-Roman ideal of the citizen-solider can be seen in the call of all Frenchmen to fight for liberty in the *levée en masse*. Given the connotations of the term in the original French, it matches much more closely the Classical principles of citizen-soldiery than a mere mass mobilization.[137] This Greco-Roman-style citizen army, therefore, harkens back to Montesquieu's Classically influenced writings. The fact that an effigy of Montesquieu was placed upon the altar of Reason during the Fête of Reason helps solidify the reality of his influence.[138]

Other figures such as Voltaire and Jacques-Louis David played important roles in the Terror. Although long dead by the time of the Reign of Terror, Voltaire's polemics against Christianity and his appeal to antiquity for undermining the Church's authority influenced the Terror's policies of dechristianization. Voltaire's claim that the religions of antiquity were more rational than that of Christianity sowed the seeds of French revolutionary government's secular state cults. His pantheonization, like that of Rousseau's, makes it difficult to refute that he had an impact upon the philosophies of the revolutionaries.[139]

David's Classical influences and their spanning from the Enlightenment into the Revolution are the most materially apparent and tangible, since he actively participated alongside Robespierre in the aesthetic policies of the Jacobin government. As the foremost Neo-Classical

---

[135] Gordon, *Montesquieu: The French Philosopher Who Shaped Modern Government*, 78.

[136] Maurice Cranston, "The French Revolution: Ideas and Ideologies," *History Today* 39, no. 5 (May 1989), http://www.historytoday.com/maurice-cranston/french-revolution-ideas-and-ideologies (accessed 22 November 2012).

[137] R. Claire Snyder, *Citizen-Soldiers and Manly Warriors*, 68.

[138] Lyttle, "Deistic Piety in the Cults of the French Revolution," 24.

[139] Ibid.

painter of his era, there is no doubt that Classicism shaped his work. Also as the art director of the Terror government, there is little doubt that his influences and work impacted Revolutionary France.[140]

The above men all were titanic figures during the Enlightenment and, later, the French Revolution. As men of such importance, their influences merit inquiry. Given the fact that they shaped the policy of the Revolution and that the works of Classical antiquity influenced their philosophies, it, therefore, stands to reason that these men operated as conduits of Classical thought into the Revolution and the Reign of Terror. This intellectual transference of Enlightenment Classicism serves as a warning as to the dangerous power of ideas, even ideas as old as Western civilization itself.

---

[140] Honour, *Neo-Classicism*, 75.

CHAPTER 2: MYSTICISM AND THE OCCULT IN *ANCIEN RÉGIME* FRANCE

Any layperson vaguely familiar with Classical aesthetics and motifs could guess that Greco-Roman culture influenced the designs of the Cults of Reason and of the Supreme Being. There is little controversy in arguing that philosophes and revolutionaries alike smiled fondly upon the cultures that birthed Plato and Plutarch. With all the supposed rationality and logic inherent in Classical influences, however, the influence of the bizarre and esoteric lurks as well.

Typically, the body of French cultural historiography depicts the early modern religious paradigm as Roman Catholicism versus Protestantism—with the loud minority of Deism, later tossed into the equation during the Enlightenment. A favorite religious topic of historians of the French Revolution, Jansenism, undoubtedly served an important political influence as criers of governmental reform reflective of the people's will, but too many historical surveys often treat the Jansenists as the most fringe religious element of the period in.[1] The reality of French religious culture, however, was not so simple.

As the historiography of the Enlightenment continues to mature past the broken model that the period was an "Age of Reason" compared to the "darkness" of the Middle Ages, more historians are beginning to delve into the irrationality hidden beneath the Enlightenment's veneer of science. As Nicholas Goodrick-Clarke's entire oeuvre of the history of Western esotericism demonstrates, the birth of modern rationalism did not kill man's inclination toward fantastical thought. The West's ancient fascination with the Occult and esotericism did not dissolve in the dawning of the Scientific Revolution. After all, "esoteric ideas often attend the breakdown of settled religious orthodoxies and socioeconomic orders," and the death of the *ancien régime*

---

[1] Sylvia Neely, *A Concise History of the French Revolution*, (Lanham, Maryland: Rowman & Littlefield, 2008), 27.

would be nothing if not a breakdown of order and orthodoxy.[2] Understanding the Occult's long

role as France's mistress while the nation officially stayed married the Catholic Church provides

insights into why many of the French flew into the arms of the state cults: many of them already

held heretical beliefs on some level.

A BRIEF HISTORIOGRAPHY OF THE OCCULT IN REVOLUTIONARY

FRANCE

Although histories focusing on Occult practices largely remain the domain of dubious

publications in bookstores' "New Age" section, sequestered away from the shelves of

"acceptable" histories, the historiographic landscape has been slowly, but surely, changing in

recent years. Christopher McIntosh surveyed France's curiosity with the Occult in *Eliphas Lévi

and the French Occult Revival*—one of the earlier attempts by an academic to venture into a

traditionally "gauche" topic. Although the crux of McIntosh's research was the nineteenth-

century's fascination with Tarot, as promoted by the infamous French ceremonial magician

Eliphas Lévi, McIntosh, nonetheless, provides insight into occultism during the Enlightenment.

For example, he highlights Court de Gébelin's immense popularity following the publication of

his multivolume series, *Le monde primitif,* in which he promotes Tarot as a surviving

compendium of encoded ancient Egyptian knowledge.[3]

Unlike the few works dedicated to Revolutionary cults and feasts, such as Mona Ozouf's

monograph, McIntosh (albeit briefly, since his analysis is only two chapters long, "The Occult

and the Revolution" and "Revolutionary Cults,") places them within the historical continuity of

---

[2] Nicholas Goodrick-Clarke, *The Western Esoteric Traditions: A Historical Introduction* (New York: Oxford University Press, 2008), location 284. Kindle edition.

[3] Christopher McIntosh, *Eliphas Lévi and the French Occult Revival* (Albany: State University of New York Press, 2011), 50.

the occult. One area of particular note in McIntosh's analysis is the role of Freemasonry lodges as catalysts for social change in the years preceding the Revolution. Masonic lodges allowed different social strata (excluding the working class, since they were not "free") to interact on relatively equal footing as members of the same fraternal organization, "a remarkable innovation considering the fossilised rigidity of social division in France at that time."[4] Lodges promoted skepticism and intellectual inquiry, but, as the latter years of the eighteenth century grew more radical against religion, McIntosh argues that the civilized discourses over brandy grew into the Revolution's dechristianization.[5]

Medievalist John V. Fleming's *The Dark Side of the Enlightenment: Wizards, Alchemists, and Spiritual Seekers in the Age of Reason* dives into everything from Rosicrucianism to alchemy. With such a wide array of subjects, Fleming focuses mainly on the Occult experience in England and Germany with discussions of the French experience intermingled. He argues that the Enlightenment wrongfully bragged of itself as the opposite of the Middle Ages' supposed "darkness."[6] Instead, Enlightenment philosophers throughout Europe nurtured the flame of Occultism, through practices such as Freemasonry, enabling the fire to flare up again in the Romantic era.[7]

One concept of particular interest in Fleming's research is that anti-Christian sentiment, such as denial of the Trinity, the Incarnation, and biblical inerrancy, made it possible for Occult hobbies and interests to survive during the Enlightenment.[8] That is, people could not entirely dismiss the possibility of the miraculous, but neither would they accept mainstream Christianity,

---

[4] Ibid., 40-41.
[5] Ibid., 42-43.
[6] John V. Fleming, *The Dark Side of the Enlightenment: Wizards, Alchemists, and Spiritual Seekers in the Age of Reason* (New York: W. W. Norton, 2013), 7-11.
[7] Ibid., 2
[8] Ibid., 16

so they turned to pseudo-religious practices such as Freemasonry, which "was indeed very much like the experience of Christianity in its social and corporate dimensions."[9] Thus, "enlightened" types would replace their experience as a member of the Gallican Church with rituals at the local masonic lodge—all the fun and none of the commitment of an actual theology.

Like the overall focus of McIntosh's work, though, the bulk of French Occult histories fixate upon the nineteenth-century, such as John Wayne Monroe's *Laboratories of Faith: Mesmerism, Spiritism, and Occulitsm in Modern France*. The few Occult histories which focus upon the eighteenth-century rarely center on France, as is the case in Paul Kléber Monod's *Solomon's Secret Arts: The Occult in the Age of Enlightenment*. Monod's title ought to be more precisely titled *The Occult in the Age of the* British *Enlightenment*, since his arguments and evidence center on the British Occult experience. If he mentions French Occultism, such as France's brief craze for mesmerism or French convulsionary fringe movements, it is within a British context.[10] Given the connectedness between British/Scottish Freemasonry and French Freemasonry, though, Monod's research provides useful insights into the development of the British fraternity in France.

At this current stage, the historiography of French esotericism and heterodoxy remains absent during the Enlightenment. To make up for the historiographic gap, this chapter shall connect the proverbial dots between the magical black market Affair of the Poisons and the séances of the nineteenth century, thereby demonstrating the continuity of heterodox belief among the French that would make acceptance of the cults possible.

---

[9] Ibid., 16, 21, 140-141.

[10] Paul Kléber Monod, *Solomon's Secret Arts: The Occult in the Age of the Enlightenment* (New Haven: Yale University Press, 2013), 204, 344.

BEGINNINGS: THE AFFAIR OF THE POISONS

Although fascination with magic and hidden knowledge has always lurked in the shadows of society, the Affair of the Poisons shall serve as this study's starting point for the analysis of modern French heterodoxy. This scandal from the Sun King's reign serves as the beginning for this analysis of beliefs outside of Gallican orthodoxy, since many surveys of the French Revolution begin with dissecting life under Louis XIV before steaming ahead into the world of Louis XVI and Marie-Antoinette. The dissection of the gamut of religious and spiritual beliefs, spanning Louis XIV's absolutism to the weakened rule of his great-great-grandson, removes the mystery as to why so many "enlightened" Frenchmen would support the new revolutionary cults. Besides the philosophical argument that man is a religious animal, the cults were possible because—to loosely borrow a philosophical concept from Chartier—the French had a history of conceiving of and believing everything from magic charms to necromancy.

THE OCCULT WORLD (AND UNDERWORLD) OF LOUIS XIV'S FRANCE

In her investigation of the underground magical services ring of seventeenth-century France uncovered during the Affair of the Poisons, *Strange Revelations: Magic, Poison, and Sacrilege in Louis XIV's France*, Lynn Wood Mollenauer illustrates the ubiquitous heterodoxy present in what would typically be classified as a "Christian nation." Recounting the testimonies from the police investigation, Mollenauer navigates the black market of sorceresses, magicians, poisoners, potion-makers, and renegade priests,[11] who earned their coin from virtually anyone

---

[11] Renegade priests were ordained Catholic priests who would moonlight as Occultists and magicians—specifically necromancers, sorcerers who specialized in summoning demons and/or spirits of dead persons. Their services were the most expensive out of all the magic black market: besides the fact that any exposure of their nefarious activities would mean certain death under the law, the French believed that their charms and rituals were the most potent of any sorcerer's. This idea stems from the French people's belief that the transfigurative powers of priests during the Eucharist could be harnessed

who could afford their services—from the middling class with extra pocket money to the dandyish court of Versailles.[12]

According to Mollenauer, what intrigued people (such as Louis XIV's favorite mistress, Madame de Montespan) toward such dubious practices was that magic offered power to those with generally little control over their own fates.[13] A woman like Madame de Montespan had great influence as the king's lover, but enjoyed little security as part of his harem—beauty, after all, does not last forever.[14] Hiring renegade priests to summon demons and wipe out her competition was one of the few ways de Montespan could experience a sense of job security.

The king's kept women, however, were not alone in using magic as a form of control in an unsure world.[15] All customers' purchasing habits reveal the extent to which people wanted control over their destinies. Magical parchments, for example, promised "to bring their possessors good luck; they ostensibly warded off the evil eye, provided protection in battle, guaranteed lawyers victory in the courtroom, and even rendered a possessor's declaration of love irresistible to whomever heard it."[16] More dubious forms of control manifested in the purchases of cuckolding wives trapped in unhappy, yet economically beneficial marriages: lining a bit of *secret du crapaud* (the sorceresses' prized toad-based poison costing upwards of 200 *louis d'or*) in the unsuspecting husband's cup spelt financial independence for the conniving wife.[17]

---

and used outside of the Church. That is, the French were so sincere in their belief in priests' ability to transform a wafer and wine into the literal body and blood of Christ, then they possessed strong magic which could enhance any spell, charm, or ceremony. For further detail, see chapter four of Mollenauer's *Strange Revelations.*

[12] Lynn Wood Mollenauer, *Strange Revelations: Magic, Poison, and Sacrilege in Louis XIV's France* (University Park, Pennsylvania: Pennsylvania State University Press, 2007), 3-4, 77.

[13] Ibid., 94-95.

[14] Ibid., 60-61.

[15] Ibid., 95.

[16] Ibid., 89.

[17] Ibid., 93-95.

More than the marginalized, however, dabbled in magical practices and products. A wide demographic swath—spanning everyone from young middleclass ladies to aged Catholic priests—practiced varying degrees of Christian heterodoxy. In Lieutenant General Gabriel Nicolas de la Reynie's investigation of a potential conspiracy to poison the Sun King, the police unearthed an entire black market of magic charms, love potions, and poisons.[18] For the right price, a wealthy client could even hire a Catholic priest to operate as a necromancer and conjure up the demon Asmodeus himself through a demonic mass.[19] La Reynie arrested and interrogated key service providers in the underground ring, such as the sorceress known as La Voisin, who named names and shared all of their (literally) gory details. The most scandalous revelation of all was that Louis XIV's chief mistress, Athénaïs de Montespan, was a prized customer of love charms and spells to secure her position as the object of the king's affections.[20]

Interestingly, the events of scandal also permeated the French psyche, even into the late eighteenth century. Grub street's pornographic ridicule of Marie-Antoinette around the Revolution frequently compared her to the mythical witch Medea and also claimed that the queen "attempted to poison her husband with a 'lethal dose of crushed diamonds.'"[21]

---

[18] Ibid., 11, 41-44, 127.

[19] Renegade priests conducted demonic masses, which were like a regular mass in church, but capped off with a spell from a grimoire (a book of magic spells and incantations), such as *Enchiridium Leonis Papae*. At the climax of the mass, a baby (miscarried, stillborn, aborted, or alive—accounts differ as to which) would be sacrificed, so the infant's blood would entice the demon to enter the ceremony's space. Clients would pay for a demonic mass for a variety of reasons, such as killing a client's enemies or entrapping the demon in a mirror so it would divine the future. Demonic masses are not to be confused with black masses, which parody the Eucharist and intend to summon Satan himself. Demonic masses, as the priests stressed during their interrogations during the Affair of the Poisons, do not parody communion. For more detail, see Mollenauer's *Strange Revelations*; she dedicates the entirety of chapter four to renegade priests' diabolical activities.

[20] Anne Somerset, *The Affair of the Poisons: Murder, Infanticide, and Satanism at the Court of Louis XIV* (New York: St. Martin's Press, 2003), 41.

[21] Mollenauer, *Strange Revelations*, 69.

Pamphleteers even accused her of poisoning her own son.[22] These fantastic accusations sprang from France's history of women, such as de Montespan, manipulating the court at Versailles through occult arts during the Affair of the Poisons.

Although there is debate regarding the veracity of some testimonies of services rendered by sorceresses and renegade priests—there is, after all, little historical science can do to prove whether or not a necromancer-priest did indeed summon a demon via infanticide for the favorite mistress of Louis XIV—the investigation highlights two disturbing facts. It demonstrates that hiring practitioners of magic and the Occult arts was in vogue during the late seventeenth-century, based on how many fashionable ladies were arrested for their connection to the Affair of the Poisons; witchcraft was alive and well in the *ancien régime*.[23] Second, the Affair revealed that the Gallican Church employed a number of renegade priests, thus even much of the Church's leadership practiced heterodoxy.[24] This lack of Christian orthodoxy in France during the seventeenth and eighteenth centuries would help create the climate conducive to the eventual creation of the state cults.

THE FRATERNAL ORDER OF FREEMASONRY

As the public sphere developed throughout Europe in the eighteenth century, so too began the need for a separate private sphere.[25] The fraternal order of Freemasonry provided men—no matter their social strata—a perfect, private alternative to public life as "a sociable

---

[22] Ibid., 161, note 120.
[23] Ibid., 159.
[24] Ibid., 45, 75, 78.
[25] Monod, *Solomon's Secret Arts*, 17.

organization that rested on vows of secrecy, mysterious rituals and an elaborate mythology of origins."[26]

Scottish rite Freemasonry gained popularity in Catholic France during the eighteenth century, despite the fact that the Roman Catholic Church distrusted Freemasons to the point that Pope Clement XII announced that membership at a lodge served as grounds for excommunication (although little was actually done to enforce the papal bull).[27] Lodges, such as the famous Neuf-Sœurs in Paris, operated as a more enclosed form of coffeehouses (i.e., a place for informed men to meet and discuss politics, philosophy, etc.).[28] Famous members of the Neuf-Sœurs include Voltaire, the abbé Sieyès, Republican calendar designer Charles-Gilbert Romme, and Occultist Antoine Court de Gébelin, who served as lodge secretary in the late 1770s.[29]

Although the first English lodges were not originally esoteric in flavor, the continental ones became intertwined during the Enlightenment with Western occult traditions, such as Hermeticism and alchemy (as well as fads such as mesmerism).[30] Like the mystical practice of alchemy, Freemasonry served as "an ethical quest based in the allegory of an artisanal technique": Freemasonry illustrated a member's journey to enlightenment through stone

---

[26] Ibid.

[27] Fleming, *The Dark Side of the Enlightenment* 138-140.

[28] Ibid., 163.

[29]"To Benjamin Franklin from Court de Gébelin, 29 June 1778," Founders Online, National Archives, http://founders.archives.gov/documents/Franklin/01-26-02-0633 (accessed March 8, 2014).

Roger Pearson, *Voltaire Almighty: A Life in Pursuit of Freedom,* (New York: Bloomsbury, 2005), 382-383.

Marie-Hélène Huet, *The Culture of Disaster* (Chicago: University of Chicago Press, 2012), 126.

Martin S. Staum, *Minerva's Message: Stabilizing the French Revolution* (Montreal: McGill-Queen's University Press, 1996), 40.

[30] Goodrick-Clarke, *The Western Esoteric Traditions,* locations 188, 2565-2574, 2754, 2911.

construction, just as alchemy's transfiguration of base metal to gold operated as a metaphor for spiritual transformation.[31] This sort of areligious spiritual improvement would have appealed to rationalist men who appreciated the moralistic benefits of organized religion, but preferred to skip the dogma and "superstition."

The French Freemasonic offshoot, the Avignon Society, infused the fraternity with mysticism, claiming that their duty was to prepare humanity for the return of Jesus Christ and His millennial reign.[32] Other French Freemasons were not as specific in their views regarding the imminent future for France, but many believed they were "an approaching age of spiritual revelation and worldwide unity, perhaps in the near future."[33]

These esoteric lodges, as Hunt highlights, contributed to the visual language of the new republic's religions.[34] Masonry borrowed visual elements from antiquity, which then influenced the Revolution's motifs, such as the Roman fasces and the laurel, as exemplified in Nicolas-Henri Jeauret de Bertry's painting of the pantheonized Rousseau, *Allégorie révolutionnaire*.[35] The Masonic singular eye of Providence, often inscribed within a pyramid, appeared on revolutionary propaganda, such as Jean-Jacques-François le Barbier's painting of the Declaration of the Rights of Man.[36]

Some pseudohistorical approaches to the Enlightenment and French Revolution shroud Freemasonry in an unnecessary nefarious shadow, such as the abbé Augustin Barruel's

---

[31] Fleming, 148, 188.

[32] Clarke Garrett, *Respectable Folly: Millenarians and the French Revolution in France and England* (Baltimore: Johns Hopkins University Press, 1975), 14-15.

[33] Ibid., 20.

[34] Hunt, *Politics, Culture, and Class in the French Revolution*, 60.

[35] Ibid.

Nicolas-Henri Jeaurat de Bertry, *Allégorie révolutionnaire*, oil on cardboard, 1794, Musée Carnavelet, Paris.

[36] Hunt, *Politics, Culture, and Class in the French Revolution*, 60.

Jean-Jacques-François le Barbier, *Déclaration des droits de l'homme et du citoyen*, oil on wood, ca. 1789, Musée Carnavelet, Paris.

conspiratorial magnum opus, *Memoirs Illustrating the History of Jacobinism.* A former Jesuit and émigré during the Revolution, Barruel penned one of the first analyses of Jacobinism's role in the French Revolution, which also was the first elaborate conspiracy theory treatise in history.[37] In his instant best-seller (in conservative England), Barruel asserted that the French Revolution stemmed from "an anti-Christian conspiracy" orchestrated by the efforts of anti-monarchialist Freemasons, the anti-Christian rhetoric of the *philosophes,* and the Bavarian Illuminati.[38] While the presence of anti-Christian rhetoric among Enlightenment philosophers such as Voltaire is undeniable, Barruel's overarching thesis rests upon misinformation, as even noted by the anti-revolutionary Edmund Burke whose own conservative leanings did not prevent him from assessing *Memoirs Illustrating the History of Jacobinism*'s conclusions as incorrect.[39] Whether or not Barruel's personal opinions and theories on the Revolution's origins were incorrect, they did nonetheless maintain a lasting impact through the centuries. "So convincing did what he produced seem to his readers, that he, more than any other person, defined the terms in which freemasonry's connexion with the Revolution is still discussed. Few objective scholars have dictated the shape of their subject for so long as this unbalanced and undiscriminating priest."[40]

In this regard, the general description of Freemasonry as "Occult" is merely a description of the society as an esoteric organization, not a moral evaluation à la Barruel. No matter the activities behind the lodges' closed doors, Freemasonry further highlights an area of French Occult culture. The fact that so many within France would participate in the lodges despite the threat of excommunication illustrates how little eighteenth-century Frenchmen feared the

---

[37] J. M. Roberts, *The Mythology of Secret Societies* (New York: Charles Scribner's Sons, 1972), 188-194.

[38] Ibid., 194.

[39] Ibid., 201.

[40] Ibid., 202.

hammer of orthodox authority. Such disregard toward the Roman Catholic Church's edicts and doctrines would make it easier for the eventual displacement of ecclesiastical authority altogether in France during the institution of the state cults.

POPULAR OCCULT PUBLICATIONS DURING THE ENLIGHTENMENT

As T. C. W. Blanning illustrates in *The Culture of Power and the Power of Culture: Old Regime Europe, 1660-1789*, the eighteenth century's rise of the public sphere was possible because of the high literacy among the French populace.[41] Cultural pursuits, such as reading the latest best-seller, no longer belonged solely to the nobility's social sphere.[42] By analyzing popular and officially published works during the years preceding the French Revolution, the public's interest in esoteric subjects becomes apparent. These literary trends aid in understanding the intellectual climate that would have made the creation of and the people's general participation in the state cults possible.

As more and more people began to consume literature, the philosophical celebrities of the day did not dominate the book market. Purchasing astrology texts, dream interpretation codices, and the like during the Enlightenment was "a trend which increased in intensity in the 1780s."[43] The wide subculture of French occult publishing delved into "many works 'hermetic, cabalistic, and theosophic philosophers, propagating fanatically all the old absurdities of theurgy, of divination, of astrology, etc.'"—avidly read by both educated and uneducated consumers alike.[44]

One example of an esoteric publication popular during the years surrounding the Revolution was the Renaissance French seer, Michel de Nostradamus's symbol-laden prophetic

---

[41] T. C. W. Blanning, *The Culture of Power and the Power of Culture: Old Regime Europe 1660-1789*, (New York: Oxford University Press, 2002), 111-112.

[42] Ibid., 181.

[43] Garrett, *Respectable Folly*, 19-20.

[44] Ibid.

quatrains. His epistle to Henry II, in which Nostradamus claimed that the Age of Saturn would return around end of the eighteenth-century, after "climactic period in world history [that] would begin in 1780 and last until 1792."[45] In 1790, the idea that Nostradamus foretold the French Revolution became a popular theory in Paris.[46]

Besides the reprinting of Nostradamus's old writings, the Occult literature market printed new material in newspapers sponsored by members of the nobility, such as Bathilde d'Orléans, the duchesse de Bourbon and funder of the *Journal prophétique*.[47] De Bourbon gained a reputation during the latter half of the eighteenth century as a mystic and supporter of the Revolution.[48] Her salon entertained the likes of Anton Mesmer and the controversial prophetess Suzette Labrousse, who claimed that the Revolution heralded that God would purify the world with the new age.[49] De Bourbon found Labrousse revolutionary prophecies especially interesting and had them published in the *Journal prophétique*.[50]

Antoine Court de Gébelin, a Protestant clergyman turned esotericist and tarot enthusiast, gained popularity on par with Rousseau in the 1780s through the publication of his nine-volume encyclopedic series, *Le monde primitif*.[51] Court de Gébelin's ambitious project aimed to discuss anything and everything related to the ancient world, with an especial interest regarding linguistics and comparative religion.[52] In his mammoth series, he covered topics such as his theory the Egyptians invented Tarot cards as a way to allegorically communicate the history of

---

[45] Clarke, *Respectable Folly*, 44-45.
Michel de Nostradamus, "Epistle to Henry II," in *Oracles of Nostradamus*, ed. Charles A. Ward (1891), http://www.sacred-texts.com/nos/oon/oon07.htm (accessed March 22, 2014).
[46] Clarke, *Respectable Folly*, 46.
[47] Ibid., 54.
[48] Ibid.
[49] Ibid., 33, 54.
[50] Ibid., 54.
[51] Edelstein, *The Terror of Natural Right*, 246.
[52] Christopher I. Lehrich, *The Occult Mind: Magic in Theory and Practice* (Ithaca, New York: Cornell University Press, 2012), 96, 138.

mankind, from the Age of Gold to the Age of Iron.[53] The first volume of Court de Gébelin's best-selling encyclopedic series, which aimed to discuss anything and everything in the ancient world, even earned him the recognition to have an audience with Louis XVI.[54] Given the difficulty authors could experience in getting officially published, because of *ancien régime* government censorship, Court de Gébelin's success would noteworthy alone for having captured the public's attention as well as the government's blessing for publication.[55] The fact was so popular despite his arcane subject manner makes him all the more intriguing.

Court de Gébelin's publications on Tarot as a tool for divination caught the attention of the mononymous cartomancer Etteilla.[56] Like Court de Gébelin, Etteilla believed that tarot served not only as a form of divination, but also contained esoteric imagery with origins in Hermeticism and ancient Egypt, as well as connections to astrology.[57] In accordance with this pseudo-historical and esoterical logic, Etteilla asserted that the tarot deck was the unbound Book of Thoth, the Egyptian equivalent of Hermes/Mercury.[58]

The anagrammatic pseudonym of Jean-Baptiste Alliette, Etteilla published the first manual of cartomancy, *Etteilla, ou manière de récréer avec un jeu des cartes,* in 1770—which gained enough popularity to demand subsequent reprintings in 1773 and 1783.[59] His writings inspired Parisian consumers' demand for Tarot packs for the first time in a century, and he

---

[53] Antoine Court de Gébelin, *Le monde primitif, analisé et comparé avec le monde moderne* (Paris: Durand, 1781), 8: 395-400.

[54] McIntosh, *Eliphas Lévi and the French Occult Revival,* 49-50.

Lehrich, *The Occult Mind,* 137.

[55] McIntosh, *Eliphas Lévi and the French Occult Revival,* 12.

Blanning, *The Power of Culture and the Culture of Power,* 137-138.

[56] McIntosh, *Eliphas Lévi and the French Occult Revival,* 50-51

[57] Helen Farley, *A Cultural History of Tarot: From Entertainment to Esotericism,* (New York: I.B. Tauris, 2009), 107-109.

[58] Ibid., 109.

[59] Ibid., 106.

capitalized upon this trend by buying decks in bulk and reselling them in the capital.[60] The

popularity of his unique decks (which, contained differing image from Court de Gébelin's

Marseilles deck) continued past the death of the *ancien régime*, as evidenced by the Etteilla Book

of Thoth decks printed during the Republican years and even into Napoleon's reign.[61]

AN ATLANTIC APPROACH TO UNDERSTANDING FRENCH HETERODOX HOBBIES

Through the analysis of the spread of Occult practices from France to its colonial jewel,

Saint Domingue, the popularity of such trends in French culture becomes even more apparent.

Their infiltration in the faraway region of the Caribbean serves as an insight into how intertwined

esotericism had become with French culture: the French populations interests in tarot,

Mesmerism, and the like had grown to be important enough that the colonists expensively

imported these Occult objects rather than do without them in the New World.

Mesmerism-mania in Enlightenment Paris and its subsequent popularity in the French

colony of Saint-Domingue offer insight into the ubiquity of occult trends in French society, both

in its cosmopolitan core and in the colonial periphery. As shown in François Regourd's study of

mesmerism's spread from Paris to Saint-Domingue in the eighteenth century, "Mesmerism in

Saint-Domingue: Occult Knowledge and Vodou on the Eve of the Haitian Revolution," Occult

---

[60] Originally, tarot was a mundane Italian card game, *tarrochi*, popular at Renaissance courts. The fad traveled to France and eventually faded during the seventeenth century. In this context, therefore, Etteilla was the first businessman/Occultist to specially market tarot cards for divination. For further information see Helen Farley's *A Cultural History of Tarot: From Entertainment to Esotericism.*

Farley, *A Cultural History of Tarot*, 109.

[61] *Petit Etteilla*, printed playing card pack, ca. 1800-1850, Paris, The British Museum, London http://www.britishmuseum.org/research/collection_online/collection_object_details.aspx?objectId=32615 12&partId=1&searchText=Etteilla&view=list&page=1 (accessed April 1, 2014).

intellectual fads transferred from the Old World to the New.[62] Regourd highlights that

mesmerism gained great popularity in the French Atlantic, and, even after its death as a fad in

Paris, the occult practice still remained generally favorable amongst Saint-Domingue's creole

population.[63] There was a delay in the advent Mesmerism's popularity in Saint-Domingue—it

arrived to the island six years after the Franz Mesmer's first dazzled curious Parisians with his

"animal magnetism"—but this temporal lag does not diminish that the French colonists desired

to remain abreast of European Occult trends enough to find the shipment of a "magnetic tub"

across the Atlantic Ocean worth the cost.[64]

As Brest in the western province of Bretagne possessed a geographic advantage as an

Atlantic port city, many colonists and sailors to Saint-Domingue hailed from this Celtic

province, and their Celtic-influenced religious culture traversed the Atlantic during the

seventeenth and eighteenth centuries.[65] Despite being an officially Catholic nation, Bretagne

exhibited pre-Christian folk magic in daily life. An example of a typical Breton superstition

entailed Breton women sweeping up the dust from the local chapel's floor, which they would

then throw up into the air to ensure that their husbands and sons would return safely from their

---

[62] François Regourd, "Mesmerism in Saint-Domingue: Occult Knowledge and Vodou on the Eve of the Haitian Revolution," in *Science and Empire in the Atlantic World*, eds. James Delbourgo and Nicholas Dew (New York: Routledge, 2008): 311-312.

[63] Ibid., 319-320.

[64] Ibid., 312.

[65] Ibid., 313.

Donald J. Cosentino, "Imagine Heaven," in *Sacred Arts of Haitian Vodou*, ed. Donald J. Cosentino (Los Angeles: UCLA Fowler Museum of Cultural History, 1995), 37.

LeGrace Beson, "Some Breton and Muslim Antecedents of Vodou Drapo," *Textile Society of America Symposium Proceedings* (January 1997): 71.

LeGrace Benson, "How Houngans Use Light from Distant Stars," *Journal of Haitian Studies* 7, no. 1 (Spring 2001): 106, 121.

fishing trip.[66] With their love of pre-Christian superstition, Breton colonists in Saint-Domingue developed the reputation for being more interested their folklore than Catholicism, to the point of even possessing a "Voltairean contempt for Church doctrine."[67]

Forms of Breton heterodoxy were prevalent enough in Saint-Domingue to permeate into the development of Vodou. Saint-Domingue's slave population exhibited a syncretism-friendly worldview and adapted the religious and Occult practices of their masters to suit their own needs. For example, popular French grimoires from the eighteenth-century appear in Vodou, such as *Le Dragon Rouge ou la Grand Grimoire* (*The Red Dragon or the Grand Grimoire*), *La Poule Noire* (*The Black Chicken*), *le Petit Albert* ("Albert" referring to the mage and saint Albertus Magus).[68] Likewise, as tarot became a favorite pastime of many French, Breton immigrants transplanted the practice to their New World abodes, which their slaves would then appropriate as an element of Vodou.[69] Bretons curious about magic and the Occult stowed the fashionable grimoires and tarot decks in their bags as they sailed across the ocean to their new lives in Saint-Domingue, which observant slaves would then appropriate as ritual fixtures in Haitian Vodou.[70]

As the pre-Christian Breton folk traditions illustrate, more than mainstream Catholicism travelled to Saint-Domingue. Folk superstitions and beliefs from Bretagne further highlight the French culture's links to its pre-Christian religious heritage.

---

[66] Stuart Clark, "Witchcraft and Magic in Early Modern Culture," in *Witchcraft and Magic in Europe: The Period of the Witch Trials,* eds. Bengt Ankarloo and Stuart Clark (Philadelphia: University of Pennsylvania Press, 1999), 100.

[67] Cosentino, "Imagine Heaven," 37.

[68] Monod, *Solomon's Secret Arts,* 12-18, 116.

Cosentino, "Imagine Heaven," 26-27.

Owen Davies, *Grimoires: A History of Magic Books* (New York: Oxford University Press, 2010), 160-161.

[69] Cosentino, "Imagine Heaven," 37.

[70] Benson, "How Houngans Use Light from Distant Stars," 106, 124.

CONCLUSION: FRANCE'S PENCHANT FOR MAGIC AND THE OCCULT

The stereotypical perception of early modern France is of an orthodox Roman Catholic nation. The reality of the matter, however—as with every area of historical inquiry—is far more complicated. From the magical black market exposed by the Affair of the Poisons to the exportation of Occult practices from France to Saint-Domingue, heterodoxy and esotericism were ironically commonplace in French life during the Age of Reason. The fact that so many people, from the middling class to the nobility, would patronize publications, such as Court de Gébelin's writings, Etteilla's tarot manual, and the *Journal prophétique,* demonstrates that fuelled their minds with more than the Classics and Christian theology. France's heterodox penchant for the Occult and magic would ultimately allow the mindset for a neo-pagan cult to be possible.

CHAPTER 3: THE MARRIAGE OF CLASSICAL IMAGERY AND ESTORICISM IN THE REVOLUTIONARY CULTS

As demonstrated in Chapters 1 and 2, the French during the Enlightenment possessed two noteworthy interests: the study of Greco-Roman civilization and curiosity towards esotericism. As anti-Christian revolutionaries moved to the forefront and demanded that a new regime called for a religion free of the *ancien régime*'s irrational taint, the new state cults exhibited traits from both of these areas. This chapter shall discuss how the amalgamation of Classicism and Occutlism produced new religious imagery, which aimed to both fill in the spiritual hole left by dechristianization while also legitimize the Republic as a divinely appointed return to man's original state during mythical pre-history.

THE LEAP INTO A NEW RELIGION: A BRIEF OVERVIEW OF THE STATE CULTS' DEVELOPMENT

How could the anti-Christian extremism of dechristianization have been allowed to pervade the new Republic? Considering the relationship between the Church and the crown during the *ancien régime*, in connection to the Revolution itself, one does not require much imagination to see how France eventually descended into a state of radical dechristianization. The Old Regime system bound the Church and state closely together.[1] Armand Jean du Plessis, Cardinal Richelieu, acted as the symbol of the *ancien régime*'s interconnection between both Church and state: he was simultaneously a cardinal, member of the nobility, and statesman.[2]

---

[1] McManners *The French Revolution and the Church*, 88, 89, 92, 118.
[2] Orlin Damayanov, "The Political Career and Personal Qualities of Richelieu," (The American University of Paris)

Thanks to the Alexandre Dumas's literary classic, *The Three Musketeers*, Richelieu is to this day still legendary for his shrewdness, authoritarian views, and political savvy.[3] With his hands on the levers of both Church and state, Richelieu is the Old Regime's system incarnate. Another example of the Siamese twin-like relationship between the First and Second Estates in *ancien régime* France was plain to the naked eye: sculptures of kings graced both the interiors and exteriors of the cathedrals littered throughout France.[4]

Considering how closely intertwined the top two percent of France's Old Regime economy were, it is not a stretch to the imagination that radical members of the Third Estate would eventually turn on the Church after they had finished sucking the marrow from the carcass of the nobility.[5] Besides the attack upon the First Estate operating as a logical conclusion to the dismantling of the Second Estate, the French Revolutionary leaders—with their avaricious reading of Rousseau's works—followed Rousseauist logic with regard to religion.[6] As mentioned previously, according to Rousseau's Romantic worldview, the Church was superstitious; the Church believed in traditions like the unenlightened concept of the divine right of kings.[7] The French Revolution erupted (amongst other reasons) because of the "unnaturalness" and "irrationality" of the Old Regime's absolutism.[8] Therefore, since the Church believed in the divine right of kings and was a major pillar of the Old Regime—and the Old Regime, as this Rousseauist syllogism established—was "irrational" and "unnatural," then the

---

http://web.archive.org/web/20091027143700/http://www.geocities.com/Paris/5972/Richelieu.html (accessed 23 April 2012).

    [3]Ibid.

[4] McManners, *The French Revolution and the Church*, 93

[5] Ibid., 92.

Kennedy, *A Cultural History of the French Revolution*, 145.

[6] Gliozzo, "The Philosophes and Religion," 273.

McManners *The French Revolution and the Church*, 87, 133-134.

[7] Lyttle, "Deistic Piety in the Cults of the French Revolution," 31.

McManners *The French Revolution and the Church*, 89.

[8] Lyttle, "Deistic Piety in the Cults of the French Revolution," 31.

Church was therefore likewise.[9] The Church, according to the revolutionaries, was therefore not the true religion, since "true religion" was "natural." By this line of thinking, the Church went against the very ideological grain of the French Revolution and must be destroyed as an enemy of the Republic.[10]

Squashing the Church from the Republic, however, left a void in the young, fledgling government.[11] Without the Gregorian calendar and its cyclical rhythm of Christian holidays and feasts, France lost a binding cultural force.[12] Dechristianization sapped shared spiritual experience offered by life under the Church's wings.[13] The hole left by dechristianization added psychological and spiritual fragmentation to France during an already fragile and volatile period for the new government. France would not be able to survive unless the whole was somehow filled and the people offered a new unifying point.[14]

Since the French revolutionary leaders blackballed Christianity as "unnatural" and anti-Republican, Christianity would not be reintroduced by the new state. Instead of reinstating a religion dedicated to the Judeo-Christian God, the new rallying point of the state cult would be *la patrie* (which translates imperfectly into English as "the fatherland"; it carries with it a much more mystical connotation, suggestive of a bond between an ethnos and its homeland).[15] This

---

[9] Gliozzo, "The Philosophes and Religion," 275.

[10] Ibid., 274.

Lyttle, "Deistic Piety in the Cults of the French Revolution," 40.

[11] McManners, *The French Revolution and the Church*, 99, 135.

Ozouf, *Festivals and the French Revolution*, 260.

[12] Lyttle, "Deistic Piety in the Cults of the French Revolution," 30-31.

McManners. *The French Revolution and the Church*, 99.

Ozouf, *Festivals and the French Revolution*, 4, 30.

[13] Lyttle, "Deistic Piety in the Cults of the French Revolution," 30-31.

McManners, *The French Revolution and the Church*, 135.

Ozouf, *Festivals and the French Revolution*, 4.

[14] Lyttle, "Deistic Piety in the Cults of the French Revolution," 30-31.

Ozouf, "Space and Time in the Festivals of the French Revolution," 375.

Ozouf, *Festivals and the French Revolution*, 9.

[15] Lyttle, "Deistic Piety in the Cults of the French Revolution." 29, 40.

nationalistic belief system, dedicated to general revelation, would be a return to natural, primitive religion, which the Romantic philosophers ever coveted.[16] How the French revolutionary leaders would implement a return to primitive religion, after centuries of ubiquitous Christian influence, offered an interesting conundrum.

To gain insight as to just what exactly primitive religion looked like, French policymakers turned to their personal libraries brimming with *philosophes'* works and Classical literature. As outlined in Chapter 1 of this research, the Enlightenment had a love affair with Greek and Roman literature. The intellectual chain of the French Revolution comprised of revolutionary leaders fed on the *philosophes*, who in turn had engorged themselves on Classical authors. Of course, though, the Republic's policymakers did not only ingest Greco-Roman second-hand, they also devoured the Classics, such as the works of the Roman historian Plutarch. He "was the most frequently read author [by men during the French Revolution] and it was through him alone that men of the Revolution knew Greek antiquity."[17] Plutarch's works, such as *Isis and Osiris*, offered, during the late eighteenth century, the only major insights into the religious practices of antiquity, because the discipline of archaeology had yet to be developed.[18] Given the fact that French policymakers were "very sensitive to the power of images," examining Plutarch's account of Classical rites and beliefs offers insights into the practices surrounding the Cult of Reason and the Cult of the Supreme Being.[19]

Gliozzo, "The Philosophes and Religion," 282.

Ozouf, "Space and Time in the Festivals of the French Revolution," 378

McManners, *The French Revolution and the Church*, 98.

Kennedy, *A Cultural History of the French Revolution*, 330, 338.

[16] Gliozzo, "The Philosophes and Religion," 274, 276.

Ozouf, "Space and Time in the Festivals of the French Revolution," 381.

Ozouf, *Festivals and the French Revolution*, 5, 260, 276.

[17] Ibid., 273.

[18] Edelstein, *Terror of Natural Right*, 184.

[19] Ozouf, *Festivals and the French Revolution*, 203.

Armed with Plutarch's histories, the French underwent a government-funded recycling program: they recycled the old ideas of primitive religion they acquired from Plutarch and refashioned them into the new cults of the state. The new state religions of the Cult of Reason and the Cult of the Supreme Being were deemed "enlightened," because they were based upon Nature and reason, not special revelation from a specific deity.[20] Such ideas, like a God revealing Himself personally through Scripture, were mere "superstition."[21]

THE CULT OF REASON AND THE CULT OF THE SUPREME BEING

The first of the cults, the Cult of Reason, had more of an atheistic, materialistic bent. This belief system denied both the existence of a personal God and the immortality of the human soul, but it nonetheless commandeered imagery from Classical antiquity. For example, in this deity-free religion, it ironically featured a goddess played by a young woman to represent the rallying point of Reason binding the French people together.[22] Although the Cult of Reason emphasized the importance of holding ceremonies in open spaces under the uninhibited sky as the ancients did, the *Fête* of Reason appropriated Notre Dame because of that Revolutionary spirit's keenness upon desecrating what was held dear in the world of the Old Regime.[23]

In the *Culte de l'Être Suprême* (the Cult of the Supreme Being)—which Robespierre founded after personally deeming the Cult of Reason a failure and nothing but atheistic hubris— the two main theological pillars were the existence of a God and immortality of the human

---

[20] Ozouf, *Festivals and the French Revolution*, 52-53, 63, 89.
Gay, "Rhetoric and Politics in the French Revolution," 666, 669, 670.
[21] Kennedy, *A Cultural History of the French Revolution*, 339.
[22] Lyttle, "Deistic Piety in the Cults of the French Revolution," 23-24.
Ozouf, *Festivals and the French Revolution*, 5, 97, 98, 101.
Schama, *Citizens*, 778.
McManners, *The French Revolution and the Church*, 101-102.
[23] Ozouf, *Festivals and the French Revolution*, 126, 127.

soul.[24] This new cult recycled much of the imagery of the Cult of Reason, such as the theatrical element of young maidens serving as proxies for a goddess figure of Reason or holding Eleusinian-esque open-air rituals on the Champ de Mars.[25] Unlike the Cult of Reason, Robespierre's pet religious project focused more heavily upon agricultural symbolism and incorporated Liberty trees.[26]

WHY NOT THE FRANKS? WHY TAKE FROM CLASSICAL RELIGION?

With the Revolutionary leaders' emphasis upon a return to "natural" government (a republic) and "natural" religion (pre-Christian beliefs), why would they choose the beliefs of a defunct, alien culture over a thousand miles away? For this new, natural France, Frankish culture seems like an obvious choice for emulation, since the Franks are the ancestors of *la France*. To the French, however, they were the progeny of Homer's world as well as Clovis I's kingdom. France viewed itself as the both figurative and literal heir of the ancient world: figuratively, because they were returning man to the political rule of Nature, just as prehistoric man supposedly once lived, and literally, because history named them of Aeneas's bloodline.

When Gregory of Tours penned his famous *History of the Franks,* he admitted to lacking a clear origin story for the Franks.[27] He did, however, share an oft-repeated rumor that the Franks originally hailed from the Danube area.[28] Long before Gregory chronicled Frankish history,

---

[24] McManners, *The French Revolution and the Church,* 86, 102-103.

[25] Lyttle, "Deistic Piety in the Cults of the French Revolution," 29-30.
Ozouf, "Space and Time in the Festivals of the French Revolution," 376-377.
Ozouf, *Festivals and the French Revolution,* 128.

[26] Ibid., 88.

[27] Edward James, *The Franks* (Oxford: Basil Blackwell, 1991), 235-236.
Gregory of Tours, *History of the Franks,* trans Ernest Brehaut (New York: Columbia University Press, 1916) 31.

[28] James, *The Franks,* 235-236.
Gregory of Tours, *History of the Franks,* 31.

however, the Roman historian Ammanius Marcellinus claimed that a group of refugee Trojans settled in Gaul.[29] This assertion by Ammanius Marcellinus probably influenced the seventh-century chronicler Fredegar's integration of Priam's family into the bloodline of the Frankish crown.[30] The anonymous author of the *Liber Historiae Francorum* elaborated upon the Trojan origin myth by claiming that King Priam[31] as the leader of the Trojans-turned-Franks; when he and his thousands of men settled in western Europe, this Trojan diaspora became known as the Franci (which supposedly meant "fierce").[32] Other versions claim that the Franks earned their name from the Trojan prince Francion (or Francus) who led the exiles to the Rhine.[33] Either way, the Merovingian Frank rule Clovis I became identified as Trojan.[34] Under the Carolingian empire, Troy became further entwined in the origin myth of the Franks in Charlemagne's coronation in 800AD, during which Bishop Dungal proclaimed the new emperor to be of Trojan extraction and, therefore, the rightful heir of the Roman Empire.[35] For Charlemagne, Trojan ancestry served to as way to legitimize his empire as the successor of Rome's glory, since Romulus, the mythical founder of Rome, himself was a descendent of Aeneas.[36]

---

[29] Michael Wood, *In Search of the Trojan War* (Berkley: University of California Press, 1998), 33.

[30] Ian Wood, *The Merovingian Kingdoms: 450-751* (New York: Longman, 1994), 33.

[31] It ought to be noted that the author of the *Liber Historiae Francorum* clearly lacked any cursory understanding of the *Aeneid*, since he (or she) switches Priam for Aeneas, claiming that Aeneas was king during the war and that Priam was a the refugee prince. For further information, see "The Frankish Myth" section of James's *The Franks*.

[32] Wood, *In Search of the Trojan War*, 34.

[33] James, *The Franks*, 235.

[34] Lewis M. Greenberg, *Let There Be Darkness: The Reign of the Swastika* (Wynnewood, Pennsylvania: Kronos Press, 1997), 7.

[35] Ibid.

[36] Ibid.

Marie Tanner, *The Last Descendant of Aeneas: The Hapsburgs and the Mythic Image of the Emperor* (New Haven: Yale University Press, 1993), 2.

To be fair, historians for millennia have named everyone from the Romans to the Hapsburgs as descended from the wandering Trojan prince.[37] As medievalist Edward James points out, all educated people in late antiquity were aware of Virgil's Trojan origin for Rome; other nations desired to copy the Trojan refuge motif in a "desire not to be seen as inferior" to the Romans.[38] For example, the British concocted a Trojan named Brutus as the founder of London (supposedly called "New Troy" during this period), as well as the progenitor of the ancient British and Welsh.[39] Centuries later, the British again would borrow Trojan motifs during the Elizabethan era. Poets lauded the virgin queen's reign as a return to a Trojan-British monarchy, calling her the "sweet remain of Priam's state: that hope springing Troy."[40] The Tudors' British or Welsh ethnicity, the poets reasoned, made Elizabeth I an heir of the myth-historical Brutus.[41] The Spanish Hapsburgs believed themselves the last descendants of Aeneas.[42] With all these claims to Trojan heritage, a ruler or people calling themselves the heirs of the lost, idyllic realm of Troy are not particularly unique.

What does, though, make all this mytho-history worthy of note is the fact that "[a]s late as the eighteenth century genealogies of the French kings beginning with Priam were still learnt by heart by French schoolchildren."[43] No matter if fact or fancy, the Trojan origin would have been cemented into the popular and cultural conscious of the French well before revolution was even conceived as a possibility. In this line of logic, therefore, the French shared a common

---

[37] Greenberg, *Let There Be Darkness*, 8.

[38] James, *The Franks*, 235-6.

[39] Ibid., 236.
Michael Wood, *In Search of the Trojan War*, 33-34.

[40] Ibid., 34.
Greenberg, *Let There Be Darkness*, 9.

[41] Michael Wood, *In Search of the Trojan War*, 33-34.

[42] Greenberg, *Let There Be Darkness*, 9.
Tanner, *The Last Descendant of Aeneas*, 145.

[43] James, *The Franks*, 236-237.

ancestry with the ancient Romans. Skipping to Classical religious motifs in the terrorist regime's move toward an original, natural state and religious cult, therefore, cut out of the middle-man of Frankish culture. The French, logically, were the heirs of the ancient traditions of Classical civilization.

IO SATURANLIA: MOTIFS OF THE ROMAN HOLIDAY IN THE CULTS

Typically, the topic of Saturnalia belongs in the realm of Classicists and the occasional Protestant fringe polemic against the more profane Christmas traditions and imagery. The Roman feast of Saturn[44], however, contributed to the mixture of emblems, motifs, and symbols of the Revolutionary religious systems—such as the Phrygian cap and Saturn's connection to the goddess of justice, Astraea.

Saturn, according to the fifth-century Roman writer Macrobius, was a great civilizer—a law-giver and teacher of the arts of agriculture and cultivation to the Italian peninsula—as well as a beloved king, but one day disappeared without a trace.[45] Virgil, in his *Aeneid*, described the reign of Saturn in Latium as "the Golden Age," a time of peace for all peoples and forever etched into mankind's psyche.[46] In his fourth Eclogue, Virgil also foretold that one day Saturn would

---

[44] For the sake of this research, the Roman Saturnalia shall be the focus instead of its original Greek version Kronia, dedicated to Saturn's Greek counterpart Kronos. There is more information available pertaining to Saturnlia, and what is known about Kronia differs little from Saturnalia, other than the calendar dates for celebrations (i.e., Saturnalia is a winter festival, while Kronia is in the summer). See Macrobius's *The Saturnalia*, Book IV, for further detail regarding Saturnalia's Greek origins.

[45] Macrobius, *The Saturnalia*, trans. Percival Vaughn Davies (New York: Columbia University Press, 1969), 58-59.

Harry Levin, *The Myth of the Golden Age in the Renaissance* (New York: Oxford University Press, 1969), 16.

[46] Virgil, *The Aeneid*, trans. A. S. Kline, VIII: lines 23-24, 28, Poetry in Translation. http://www.poetryintranslation.com/PITBR/Latin/VirgilAeneidVIII.htm (accessed March 10, 2014).

return, call back the goddess of justice Astraea to earth,[47] and a second Golden Age would begin worldwide.[48]

Saturn's eponymous feast Saturnalia began as a way to commemorate and replicate Saturn's mythical, primordial rule.[49] To sum up the festivities of this winter solstice feast, Rome would experience "opposite day" (i.e., social norms and practices would be temporarily loosened and reversed).[50] Slaves and masters were no longer of two separate social strata during Saturnalia; sometimes their roles were even reversed, as illustrated in Horace's *Satires*, in which the poet's slave delivers the lecture instead of the poet himself.[51] In fact, Saturnalia so blurred in the lines between slaves and freemen that anyone could "speak as one wished" without fear of backlash, as well as revel in gluttony and drunkenness.[52] With the topsy-turvy nature of Saturnalia's momentary abolishment of defined social hierarchy, this major Roman festival nodded to the equality man experienced in the Age of Saturn.

Although Edelstein analyzes the Golden Age's influence on political philosophy during the eighteenth century and especially the Terror, instead of its manifestation in the Greco-Roman festivals, he does note that the myth held intellectual currency because it suggested that man's original, ideal state was equality, not under monarchial rule.[53] In understanding the Golden Age

---

[47] More detail about Astraea (also known as Dikē) below in "Astraea: The Virgin and the Scales."

[48] Edelstein, *The Terror of Natural Right,* 12.

Virgil, "Eclogue IV," in *Eclogues, Georgics, Aeneid,* trans. H.R. Fairclough (Cambridge, Massachusetts: Harvard University Press, 1916), lines 6-7. http://www.theoi.com/Text/VirgilEclogues.html#4 (accessed February 10, 2014).

Levin, *The Myth of the Golden Age in the Renaissance,* 17.

[49] Ibid., 16.

[50] Harry B. Evans, "Horace, *Satires* 2.7: Saturnalia and Satire," *The Classical Journal* 73, no. 4 (April-May 1978): 307.

[51] Ibid.

[52] Ibid.

Fanny Dolansky, "Celebrating the Saturnalia: Religious Ritual and Roman Domestic Life" in *A Companion to Families in the Greek and Roman Worlds,* ed. Beryl Rawson (Oxford: Blackwell, 2011), 492.

[53] Edelstein, *The Terror of Natural Right,* 12, 87.

myth as mirrored in Saturnalia's traditions, the revolutionary symbols of the *bonnet rouge* and various goddess figures gain an extra layer in their interpretation beyond Classical imagery appropriated by the new regime. As the next sections shall discuss, the Saturnalian motifs in the cults served as reminders of man's original state and that the French Republic's destiny was to rebirth this idyllic era.

ASTRAEA: THE STARRY GODDESS AND THE FLUIDITY OF MYTH

Goddess imagery featured prominently in the iconography of the French Revolution. Lynn Hunt's landmark work, *Politics, Culture, and Class in the French Revolution,* discusses Marianne's role as a theoretical replacement for the Virgin Mary (i.e., Hunt turns to the argument that "Marianne was semantically close to Mary") and her general popularity as a symbol throughout Revolutionary France.[54] Although she mentions Marianne's role as a multi-faceted goddess of the Republic, Hunt acknowledges this briefly and without much analysis as to her Greco-Roman origins.[55] Similarly, Mona Ozouf focuses on the impact of the goddess imagery in the festivals rather than her symbolic roots.[56] Looking at the goddess's origins in and imagery from the Golden Age goddess of Astraea, however, enables a fuller interpretation of the goddess motif in the Republic, while also further establish the importance of the Saturnian myth in the revolutionary religions.

As outlined previously regarding the myth of the Golden Age, Astraea[57] lived among mankind during Saturn's reign.[58] When mankind spiraled into sinfulness and began loving war,

---

[54] Hunt, *Politics, Culture, and Class in the French Revolution,* 93-94.

[55] Ibid., 65.

[56] Ozouf, *Festivals and the French Revolution,* 102-103.

[57] Astraea (or, Astraia, in Greek) possesses many monikers, as is often the case with ancient mythological figures, including "the Starry Maiden" (for her association with the zodiacal constellation Virgo, the virgin), Dikē/Dicē, and Justitia (for more information see Helene E. Roberts's section on

her exodus from earth marked the end of humanity's cohabitation with the gods, and she then abided in heavens as the constellation Virgo—next to the zodiac sign Libra, the scales, which also symbolized Astraea's association with justice.[59] Astraea's return to earth would mark the rebirth of the Golden Age, and humanity would again live in its natural state of equality and peace, according to Virgil's prophecy in his fourth Eclogue.[60] She would begin, to borrow biblical phraseology, "a new heaven and a new earth," for "[u]nder her protection thrives all that is noble, beautiful, and good."[61]

Although Astraea is not as famous or iconic a member of the Greco-Roman pantheon as, say, Apollo, she was not unfamiliar to educated Frenchmen in the eighteenth century. Her presence in Classical literature would have prevented her from being a foreign entity to anyone well-read. As argued in Chapter 1 of this research, the *philosophes* and revolutionary leaders were no strangers to Greco-Roman literature. Dan Edelstein, in his study of the Golden Age myth's relation to political philosophy during the Terror, *The Terror of Natural Right*, also highlights that policy-makers were familiar with Ovid's *Metamorphoses* as well as Virgil's *Eclogue* and *Aeneid*—which all reference Astraea.[62] In fact, Voltaire makes a direct reference to her in the first lines of his poem *Le Mondain*:

> Regrettera qui veut le bon vieux temps,
> Et l'âge d'or, et le règne d'Astrée,
> Et les beaux jours de Saturne et de Rhée,
> Et le jardin de nos premiers parents;

Justice in *Encyclopedia of Comparative Iconography: Themes Depicted in Works of Art*). For the purposes of this study, Astraea shall be the preferred nomenclature, since that is how Virgil refers to her, as well as various *philosophes* such as Voltaire.

[58] Ovid, *Metamorphoses,* trans. Anthony S. Kline (2000), I: lines 149-150, The Ovid Collection at University of Virginia, http://ovid.lib.virginia.edu/trans/Metamorph.htm (accessed March 2, 2014).

[59] Helene E. Roberts, ed., *Encyclopedia of Comparative Iconography: Themes Depicted in Works of Art* (Chicago: Fitzroy Dearborn, 1998), 913.

[60] Virgil, "Eclogue IV," lines 6-11.

[61] Helene E. Roberts, ed., *Encyclopedia of Comparative Iconography*, 913.

[62] Edelstein, *The Terror of Natural Right*, 12-13.

> Moi je rends grâce à la nature sage
> Qui, pour mon bien, m'a fait naître en cet âge[63]

Besides her presence in Greco-Roman literature, Astraea-Justice had been part of Western visual language since ancient times. For millennia, a woman bearing scales has served as the symbol of justice—sometimes for illustrating a mythical event or astrological reference, or perhaps both.[64] Court de Gébelin identified her,[65] in the eighth volume of his best-selling series *Le monde primitif,* as the queen depicted in the tarot card Justice, because of her sword and scales.[66] As mentioned in the previous chapter, Court de Gébelin and tarot grew in popularity during the latter half of the eighteenth-century, so his discussion of Astraea would not have fallen upon deaf ears. To further illustrate the prevalence (and uniformity) of Astraea-Justice in the visual vernacular of the eighteenth-century before the Revolution, Justice's portrayal in volume three of Hubert François Gravelot and Charles Nicolas Cochin's *Iconologie* matches the image of the Marseilles Tarot's picture of seated *la Justice*—even the tiara.[67]

This same Libran motif of Astraea appears on Louis le Coeur's print illustration, *La Constitution française.*[68] Loaded with revolutionary symbolism—such as the *bonnet rouge,* fasces, and the Constitution placed on twin tablets à la the Ten Commandments—this image of a

---

[63] Loosely translated: "Nostalgia for the good old days, / And the Golden Age, and the reign of Astraea / and the beautiful days of Saturn and Rhea [his wife], / And the garden of our first parents; / I give my thanks to wise Nature / Who, for my good, gave birth to me in this age". For the full poem (in the original French), see http://www.udel.edu/braun/poetry/voltaire.html.

Edelstien, *The Terror of Natural Right,* 88.

[64] Ami Ronnenberg and Kathleen Martin, eds., *The Book of Symbols* (Cologne, Germany: Taschen, 2010), 512.

[65] Transcribed as, *"La Justice. C'est une Reine, c'est Astrée assise sur son Trône, tenant d'une main un poignard ; de l'autre, une balance."*

[66] Court de Gébelin, *Le monde primitif,* 8: 372.

[67] Hubert François Gravelot and Charles Nicholas Cochin, *Iconologie par figures, ou, Traité complet des allegories, emblêms, &c. : ouvrage utile aux artistes, aux amateurs, et pouvant servir à la l'education des jeunes personnes* (Paris: Le Pan, 1791), 3: 29.

[68] Louis le Coeur, *La Constitution française,* colored engraving, ca. 1791-1792, Bibliothèque nationale de France, Paris.

proposed monument does not boast the image of Reason nor Liberty as the new laws' patroness.

Instead, Astraea, easily identified by her tiara, sword, and scales, serves as the Constitution's

celebrity endorsement. Her presence in the birthing of the new republic suggests the beginning of

the new Golden Age as Virgil foretold, as any Frenchman with a Classical background would be

aware.

Astraea also appeared during the French Revolution on the dechristianized Republican

calendar. She appears seated with her scales, near the personification of Time (who is also fitted

with Saturnian elements such as the scythe, which recalls Saturn's role as the first teacher of

agriculture)[69] on J.F. Lefevre's *Calendrier national*.[70] Her presence on the calendar is not simply

gratuitous, because Astraea also bore a connection to the orderliness of the seasons.[71] Her

presence next to the Saturnian figure of Time may also be an allusion to Astraea's role in the

Golden Age of Saturn, although that is up to interpretation.

Astraea's symbolism also manifests in a less literal form upon Philip-Louis Debucourt's

calendar for Year III.[72] Careful inspection of the calendar reveals the astrological symbol for

Libra (♎) underneath "Vendémiaire," the first day of which is 22 September on the Gregorian

calendar. This date holds significance because it marks the beginning of Libra's period in the

sun's astral house.[73]

---

[69] As *Iconologie* points out under its section for *Temps*, Time, in the Western tradition, contains Saturnian image because *"le Temps détruit tout"* (Time destroys all), just as Saturn/Kronos devoured his own children in the hope to maintain his supremacy.

[70] J.F. Lefevre, *Calendrier national calculé pour 30 ans et présenté à las Convention Nationale en décembre, 1792*, engraving, 1792, Musée Carnavalet, Paris.

[71] Helene E. Roberts, ed., *Encyclopedia of Comparative Iconography*, 913.

[72] Philibert-Louis Debucourt, *Calendrier républicain*, engraving, 1794, Bibliothèque nationale de France, Paris.

[73] When a zodiacal constellation enters the sun's house, this means, that during a certain period of days during the year, the sun will appear to match up with that constellation from the perspective of Earth. It is important to bear in mind that astrology views the zodiacal stars as a belt around Earth and that all the planets (to astrologers, this includes the sun and Earth's moon) move around this belt. The key point to bear in mind is that the autumnal equinox is important because it marks the switch from Virgo to Libra.

Upon, first glance it would make sense to assume the date's importance came from the fact that it was "the anniversary of the proclamation of the Republic."[74] Commemorating this key revolutionary event, however, was not the purpose of starting the calendar on the twenty-second. Charles-Gilbert Romme, chairman of the committee for the Republican calendar and member of *Les Neuf-Sœurs* lodge, chose it because 22 September because it was the autumnal equinox; that date just "happened, by a happy coincidence, to be the anniversary."[75] The autumnal equinox gains its symbolic significance not merely from the fact that day and night have equal measure on that date, otherwise the vernal equinox could have easily been chosen since the same phenomenon happens then as well. Possibly influenced by his masonic lodge-brother, the esotericist Court de Gébelin, Romme chose the twenty-second because it was the cusp between Virgo and Libra, so the new Republic would begin every year under her *balance*.[76] The calendar would also end under her constellation as well (as noted by the fact that Virgo's sign (♍) lies beneath Fructidor on Philibert-Louis Debucourt's *Calendrier*), since, as previously mentioned, the Greco-Roman mythographers record that she fled to the heavens to become the sign Virgo.[77]

Further inspection of Debucourt's calendar for the Year III further bolsters this theory of Astraea's astrological themes in the new regime's dating system. In the engraving, the goddess (identified as Philosophy) enthroned atop the calendar tramples "superstition" and reads the book

---

For further reference on the dynamics of sun signs in astrology, see *Llewellyn's Complete Book of Astrology* by Kris Brandt Rinke.

[74] Zamoyksi, *Holy Madness*, 63.

[75] Jean Ehrard, dir., *Gilbert Romme (1750-1795) et son temps, actes du colloque de Riom et Clermont* (Société des études robespierristes, 1996), 117-118.

Zamoyski, *Holy Madness*, 63.

[76] Edelstein, *The Terror of Natural Right*, 183-184, 214.

"To Benjamin Franklin from Court de Gébelin, 29 June 1778," Founders Online.

[77] Aratus, *Phaenomena*, trans. A. W. Mair and G. R. Mair, lines 96 ff, in *Theoi* http://www.theoi.com/Titan/Astraia.html (accessed February 15, 2014).

Philibert-Louis Debucourt, *Calendrier republicain*, engraving, 1794, Bibliothèque nationale de France, Paris.

of Nature, as she points her quill to the zodiacal signs presented upon the open page in the order mirroring the Republican calendar's timeline (e.g., Libra (♎), Scorpio (♏), Sagittarius (♐), etc.).[78] Through this imagery, Debucourt suggested that Libra's period in the sun is the most rational and natural beginning for the new calendar. Debucourt further asserts this point with the cherubic putto next to Philosophy. Identified as Philosophy's genius, the cherubic figure writes upon a scroll resting upon a globe with a shallow relief of the zodiac, Libra's scales in clear view.[79] Careful inspection of the scroll reveals more of the calendar's emphasis on beginning the new era in *la signe de la Balance*.[80]

Placing Astraea's astrological symbolism at the beginning of the Republic new epoch aided in cementing the idea that the French Revolution marked the beginning of the second Golden Age. Edelstein points out that Robespierre himself proclaimed that "the French people had recalled Astraea, goddess of justice."[81] While Edelstein takes a more politically symbolic interpretation of Robespierre's statement (i.e., more of an assessment of the triumph of "Golden

---

[78] In the text at the bottom of the composition, Debucourt's inscription has been transcribed as:

Sur un Sommet élevé, la Philosophie assise sur un siege de marbre décoré des images de la Nature féconde, et ayant pour Diadême le bonnet de la Liberté, foule a ses pieds les gothiques monumens derreur et de superstition sur lesquels etoit fondée l'ignorante et ridicule division destems[?]*, et puise dans le grand livre de la Nature, les principes et les denominations du nouveau Calendrier, que près d'elle un génie atentif* [sic.] *a sa voix trace sous sa dictée. De l'autre coté sont ses divers attributs telsque le livre de Morale, la Régle, et un Nouveau emblem de l'Egalité.*

[79] That is, in the Roman sense, a genius (*un génie*) was like a "guardian angel," a protective spirit "who prompted [the individual within its care] to good and noble deeds." Eventually, Roman *genii* became intertwined with Greek *Dæmons*, which "were believed to be spirits of the righteous race which existed in the Golden Age, who watched over mankind, carrying their prayers to the gods, and the gifts of the gods to them." This connection between *genii* and *Dæmons*, therefore, provides some interesting food for thought regarding the Golden Age connection of the putto in the engraving to the Golden Age imagery associated with Astraea and Libra. For more information on *Genii*, see E. M. Berens's entry on them in *The Myths and Legends of Ancient Greece and Rome.*

[80] The tiny text transcribes as: *L'Ere des Français compte de la Fondation de la Republique 22* [Sept.?] *1792 de l'ère vulgare jour ou le Soleil est entré dans le signe de la Balance...* The remaining lines describe the division of the year into months, weeks, and days.

[81] Edelstein, *The Terror of Natural Right*, 87.

Age republicanism" versus monarchy), the ideological-religious convictions exhibited by the cults and their imager suggest—as the corpus of this research asserts—less of politics and more of France's "divine role" as heralds of a reborn era of *liberté, egalité, et fraternité.*

LES TROYENS: THE PHRYGIAN CAP

One signature item of Saturnalia that is of particular note to this study is the *pilleus*, a conical hat signifying a freeman.[82] Slaves would often don the *pilleus*, which looks like the Phrygian cap, during Saturnalia as part of the freedom and role reversal celebrated during the festivities, because slaves were normally forbidden from wearing a head covering.[83] Outside of the context of Saturnalia, "when a slave was freed, he would be ceremonially coiffed with a cap by his master."[84]

Fast-forwarding from Mediterranean antiquity to eighteenth-century France, the rouge Phrygian cap supplanted the scarlet *pilleus* as the symbolic chapeau of choice for revolutionaries. It is important to note, though, that the *pilleus* and Phrygian cap are not identical, so to assert that the eighteenth-century French artists and clothing designers merely "confused" the one for the other is unlikely. The Phrygian cap is longer, bulbous, and baggier compared to the short, conical *pilleus*. A twenty-first century analogy would be comparing the iconic Smurfs' cap to a traditional birthday party hat: there is a clear difference in form, although they both are novelty headwear. According to Adam Zamoyski in *Holy Madness: Romantics, Patriots, and Revolutionaries, 1776-1871,* French artists preferred the Phrygian cap's voluminous form—as

---

[82] Dolansky, "Celebrating the Saturnalia," 492.
[83] Ibid.
Adam Zamoyski, *Holy Madness*, 59.
[84] Ibid.

seen in "ancient representations of Paris and Ganymede"[85]—to that of the *pilleus*, because the Roman hat looked awkward upon the skull, like wearing a miniaturized dunce's cap with a rounded point.[86] The elegance of the Phrygian cap, however, would command greater respect.

In 1790, the Phrygian cap first entered the visual language of the Revolutionary fêtes.[87] Educated Frenchmen were already familiar with the meaning of this red hat made of felted wool before it became a popular, political fashion statement.[88] As Nicola J. Shilliam points out in her article, "'Concordes Nationales and Bonnets Rouges': Symbolic Headdresses of the French Revolution," traditionally, slaves during the Hellenistic period were from Asia Minor—such as the neighboring states of Phrygia and Troy—and their signature hat became visual shorthand for identifying Easterners (and especially Trojans) in Hellenistic and, later, Roman art.[89]

As mentioned previously, Greco-Roman artists traditionally costumed Paris with his trademark Phrygian cap; his wearing of the hat is one of its most iconic usages in art history, perhaps second only to Mithras.[90] The Phrygian cap is so emblematic of Paris that art historians have been able to identify Paris as the subject of a Roman marble nude copy of a fourth-century BC Greek sculpture, because of the figure's lone accessory—the bonnet—as an iconographic marker.[91] Over a thousand years later, David continued the tradition and identified the young

---

[85] Zeus's homoerotic cupbearer.

[86] Zamoyski, *Holy Madness*, 59.

[87] Albert Mathiez, *Les origines des cultes révolutionnaires (1789-1792)* (Paris: Libraire Georges Bellais, 1904), locations 537-538. Kindle edition.

[88] Nicola J. Shilliam, "'Concordes Nationales and Bonnets Rouges': Symbolic Headdresses of the French Revolution," *Journal of the Museum of Fine Arts, Boston* 5 (1993): 115.

[89] Ibid.

Susan Woodford, *The Trojan War in Ancient Art*, (Ithaca, New York: Cornell University Press, 1993), 41.

[90] Ibid.

[91] "Statue of Paris, known as the Landsdowne Paris," *Louvre Museum*, http://www.louvre.fr/en/oeuvre-notices/statue-paris-known-lansdowne-paris?sous_dept=1 (accessed March 15, 2014).

prince plagued with "amorous weakness" by costuming him with little else than a rosy Phrygian cap in the lesser-celebrated oil painting, *Paris and Helen*.[92]

As Albert Mathiez highlighted in *Les origines des cultes révolutionnaires, le bonnet phrygien*, an early and ubiquitous symbol of revolutionary patriotism, first appeared upon Liberty's head in the city of Troyes.[93] Interestingly, the French adjective to describe something or someone as "of Troyes" is *troyen* (or *troyenne*, in the feminine form) is the exact same word for "Trojan" in French.[94] Given France's history of self-identifying as neo-Trojans, it seems unlikely that the unveiling of Liberty sporting a cap associated with Troy in Troyes was a mere coincidence—nor was it part of some grand connection between Troyes and Homer's Troy.

The etymological roots of Troyes reveals that the city's Latin original name, Civitas Tricassium, derived from the area's native Gallic inhabitants, the Tricasses.[95] Their name meant roughly "those with three locks of hair" (or "three tresses"), referring to the tribe's preferred coiffure of three braids.[96] Over the centuries, Civitas Tricassium evolved into Troyes, which still maintains the city's connections to the hairstyle allusion, because "Troyes" is related to *trois* (the number "three" in French).[97] Thus, a Trojan hat did not necessarily appear in Troyes because of some mystical-symbolic connection to Priam's kingdom.[98] Arguably, jumping to that conclusion would be like assuming *troi* and Troie are related because they also sound the same. Keeping Occam's razor in mind, therefore, it is safe to deem that the first utilization of the Phrygian cap

---

[92] Yvonne Korshak, "Paris and Helen by Jacques-Louis David: Choice and Judgment on the Eve of the French Revolution," *The Art Bulletin* 69, no. 1 (March 1987): 111.

[93] Matheiz, *Les origines des cultes révolutionnaires (1789-1792)*, location 538. Kindle edition.

[94] *Troie* is French for Troy. *Troie* and Troyes are homophones.

[95] Adrian Room, *Place Names of the World: Origins and Meanings of the Names for 6,600 Countries, Cities, Territories, Natural Features, and Historic Sites*, 2nd ed. (Jefferson, North Carolina: McFarland, 2005), 383.

[96] Ibid.

[97] *Trois* and Troyes are also homophones and share the Latin root for "three."

[98] "Not necessarily," because, as Adrian Room's etymological research demonstrates, the spelling of Troyes *may* have been influenced by Troy. Other than conjecture, though, there etymologists, linguists, and historians have little evidence to directly connect Troyes with Troy.

upon Liberty at Troyes was most likely a pun of sorts (e.g., Liberty wore a *troyen* hat in front of the *troyens*, the citizens of Troyes), and not "proof" of a grander connection between Priam's realm and a particular city in northern France. If anything, the appearance of the cap in Troyes was a clever play by the image's artistic director. The incident also illustrates how commonplace the knowledge of the Trojan bonnet was in eighteenth-century France (at least for those educated enough to possess a familiarity with Classical civilization) in order for such a visual "joke" to be made before a mass audience.

HERO CULTS AND *LE PANTHÉON*

The elements of Greek religion Plutarch recorded, and that the leaders of the French Revolution would have read, included the concept of hero cults. For example, in his account of the life of Theseus, Plutarch mentions the establishment of a cult dedicated in honor to the mortal hero after he achieved great acclaim for his feats of daring and saving his city-state of Athens from oppression from the kingdom of Minos.[99] Although Theseus was a man, after his death, the Athenians erected a temple dedicated to him and even offered sacrifices to him like a god.[100] Cicero, in his *De Natura Deorum,* also mentions the Greco-Roman tradition of deifying mortals, citing Hercules, Romulus, and Aesculapius, the holy healer.[101] Likewise, Hermes Trismegistus, and Agamemnon—to name a few other apotheosized mortals—enjoyed posthumous cult status.

---

[99] Plutarch, "Theseus," trans. John Dryden, http://classics.mit.edu/Plutarch/theseus.html (accessed 24 April 2012).

[100] Ibid.

[101] Cicero, *De Natura Deorum,* trans. H. Rackman (Loeb Classical Library, 1933), XIX: 323. http://penelope.uchicago.edu/Thayer/E/Roman/Texts/Cicero/de_Natura_Deorum/3A*.html (accessed February 25, 2014).

Some hero-gods, even overtook the temples of established gods, such as the case of

Agamemnon's appropriation of a temple initially dedicated to Hera.[102]

Like Theseus in Plutarch's account, the heroes of the French Revolution developed their

own posthumous cults as well. Voltaire was the first *philosophe*[103] to be interred in the Panthéon,

formally the church of Sainte-Geneviève, patron saint of Paris. The burial of one of the most

notorious critics of the Church of the modern era into hallowed ground was a distinct religious

and political statement by the revolutionary government.[104] When the government transported St.

Genviève's relics to the nearby church of Saint-Etienne-du-Mont in order to rededicate her

church as the Panthéon, devoted Catholics raised their fervent criticism of the profaning of their

holy site and relics.[105] Unfortunately for these Catholics, the Republic's Panthéon committee

ultimately decided to melt down countess-saint's coffin for its gold and mock her relics as

unmiraculous old bones,[106] with the blessings of the lower classes and *sans-culottes* disgusted by

feudalist imagery associated with St. Geneviève.[107] With St. Geneviève removed, Voltaire's

---

[102] Carla M. Antonaccio, *An Archaeology of Ancestors: Tomb Cult and Hero Cult in Early Greece* (Lanham, Maryland: Rowman & Littlefield, 1995), 150.

[103] He was not, however, the first person ever to be interred there once the church became refashioned into the Panthéon. That distinction belongs to the comte de Mirabeau, however, his funeral occurred on April 4, 1791, before the Republic even called for a state cult to replace the Christianity. For this reason, this study shall follow the lead of the majority of historians, who usually dismiss Mirabeau's pantheonization due to its heavy Catholic flavor. For further information see Suzanne Glover Lindsay's *Funerary Arts and Tomb Cult: Living with the Dead in France, 1750-1870.*

[104] Raymond Anthony Jonas, *France and the Cult of the Sacred Heart: An Epic Tale for Modern Times* (Berkeley: University of California Press, 2000), 72-73.

[105] Richard Clay, "Saint Geneviève, Iconoclasm, and the Transformation of Signs in Revolutionary Paris," in *Striking Images, Iconoclasms Past and Present,* ed. Stacy Boldrick, Leslie Brubaker, and Richard Clay (Burlington, Vermont: Ashgate, 2013), 105.

[106] Later, in 1793, as Jonas states in *France and the Cult of the Sacred Heart: An Epic Tale for Modern Times*, "Geneviève's relics would be burned on the Place de Grève in a fit of iconoclasm."

[107] Clay, "Saint Geneviève, Iconoclasm, and the Transformation of Signs in Revolutionary Paris," 106-107.

ashes were transported to the Panthéon "in a magnificent procession" during the Festival of Voltaire in July 1791.[108]

Images of Voltaire's veneration depict him beyond "saint-like," as many historians have suggested regarding the veneration paid to the sharp-tongued *philosophe* and pantheonization figures.[109] The engraving *Apothéose de Voltaire* depicts the Greco-Roman pantheon welcoming the old philosopher with open arms, as Ceres-Astraea (this winged woman bears a sheaf of wheat while also depicted next to Libra's scales) writes Voltaire's name in the heavens.[110] Although, apotheosis imagery is not unique to French Revolutionary devotional culture—George Washington even has his own allegorical apotheosis scene in the Capitol Rotunda—this type of imagery is not comparable to that of Catholic saints: they do not have their names written in the heavens next to the zodiacal wheel upon canonization. Likewise, Voltaire's glowing bust in *Constitution républicaine décretée par la Convention naitonale, l'an 2me de la liberté* takes the literal compositional center-stage between two goddess figures (one could be identified potentially as Dikē-Astraea for wielding the sword of justice), as a dove reminiscent of the Holy Spirit's iconography carries a laurel wreath aloft in its beak.[111] Although some strong-opinioned Protestants might argue that Catholics worship saints like gods, saints do not take precedence over (nor hold equal standing) in the visual language of Catholic art.[112] Instead, these images of Voltaire hearken back to Classical examples, such as the Column of Antoninus Pius, the relief-

---

[108] Jonas, *France and the Cult of the Sacred Heart*, 74.
Warren Roberts, *Jacques-Louis David and Jean-Louis Prieur: Revolutionary Artists* (Albany: State University Press of New York, 2000), 278.
[109] Clarke, *Respectable Folly*, 78.
[110] *Apothéose de Voltaire*, engraving, ca. 1791, Bibliothèque nationale de France, Paris.
[111] *Constitution républicaine décretée par la Convention naitonale, l'an 2me de la liberté*, engraving, 1793, Bibliothèque nationale de France, Paris.
[112] Of course, there is some debate regarding imagery of the Virgin Mary in relation to Jesus in some depictions, but that is another matter. For the sake preventing too many intellectual tangles, saints (e.g., Thomas, John the Evangelist, Paul the Apostle, etc.) minus the Virgin Mary are the focus for this point.

sculpted base of which depicts the deceased Roman emperor whisked up to the gods' abode to become another ruler worshipped by citizens in the imperial cult.[113]

Although little information is available regarding this *fête* for the celebrated *philosophe*—and it took place two years before the Festival of Reason in Notre Dame—it merits mention because it was the one of first revolutionary festivals David artistically spearheaded.[114] Voltaire's festival served a medium for many of David's iconographic and aesthetic contributions to the new regime's culture, which he infused with antique elements (e.g., costumes, props, etc., for "the festival's *mise en scène*") he observed during his artistic education in the Eternal City.[115] David's ancient artistic preferences for Revolutionary imagery would also manifest in later *fêtes*, such as the Festival of Reunion two years later.[116]

Unlike Voltaire, Jean-Paul Marat polarized revolutionaries. Interestingly, when Charlotte Corday stabbed Marat to death in his bathtub, Robespierre did not want to capitalize upon the funeral as a chance for another unifying ceremony for the French people.[117] Marat's cult of personality during his life made the Jacobins uncomfortable as it was, so the idea of cementing his iconic status in death only agitated that jealousy further.[118]

Nonetheless, Marat attained messianic status in his death through David's choice to pose the assassinated pamphleteer à la Michelangelo's *Pietà*, in order to liken him to the crucified figure of Christ.[119] Unlike Michelangelo's *Pietà* and other depictions of Christ's deposition from

---

[113] *Apotheosis of Emperor Antoninus Pius and Faustina*, white marble, 161 AD, Vatican Museums, Rome.

[114] Warren Roberts, *Jacques-Louis David and Jean-Louis Prieur*, 278.

[115] Ibid.

[116] Dan Edelstein, *The Terror Natural Right*, 185.

[117] Thomas Crow, *Emulation: David, Drouais, and Girodet in the Art of Revolutionary France*, rev. ed. (New Haven: Yale University Press, 2006), 163.

[118] Ibid.

[119] Fred S. Kleiner, *Gardner's Art Through the Ages: A Global History*, 13th ed. (Boston: Wadsworth, 2011), 769.

the Cross, this secularized martyrdom contains no mourners or grand background elements:

David painted Marat dead, cold, and alone in his sparse apartment.[120] Marat's nudity in the tub

also likens him to "the statues of classical heroes and dying philosophers, especially Socrates and

Seneca (who had committed suicide in his bath)," thereby connecting him to Classical martyrs of

rationalism.[121] David's infusion of Christian and Greco-Roman motifs into the painting was not

merely empty propaganda or his airing of his personal feelings toward the propagandist. The

French people latched onto Marat's posthumous divinity, writing litanies in his praise; even his

bathtub and removed heart eventually achieved holy status akin to a medieval saint's relic.[122]

Eventually, "[v]irtually all of the Republic's forty thousand or so communes had erected a

monument to him on which invocations were said."[123]

With regard to Rousseau's iconic status, he, too, gained a cult of his own. His long-dead

remains were exhumed and then removed to Sainte-Geneviève's a mere twenty days after

Marat's pantheonization.[124] Ironically, removing Rousseau to Paris violated his last will, in

which he clearly stated he desired a rural burial, in order to avoid internment in the French

capital, "the city he loathed."[125] Whatever Rousseau's wishes for his remains, he became

apotheosized into an immortalized patron of the Revolution.

Jeaurat de Bertry's previously mentioned oil painting, *Allégoire révolutionnaire*,

highlights Rousseau's posthumous role as a revolutionary demigod.[126] What makes Bertry's

---

[120] Honour, *Neoclassicism*, 155-156.

[121] Ibid.

[122] McManners, *The French Revolution and the Church*, 98.

François Gendron, *The Gilded Youth of Therimdor* (Montreal: McGill-Queen's University Press, 1993), 62.

[123] Ibid.

[124] Ozouf, *Festivals and the French Revolution*, 119.

[125] Jonathan Israel, *French Revolutionary Ideas: An Intellectual History of the French Revolution from* The Rights of Man *to Robespierre* (Princeton: Princeton University Press, 2014), 174.

[126] Nicolas-Henri Jeaurat de Bertry, *Allégorie révolutionnaire*, oil on cardboard, 1794, Musée Carnavelet, Paris.

composition striking is not the fasces-cum-liberty pole juxtaposed next to a sapling liberty tree at occupying the lower half of the painting or the symbolic half-constructed Classical architecture in the background. The image's symbolic importance comes the oval portrait of Rousseau mounted above the singular eye of Providence resting between two Republican flags. This juxtaposition within Jeaurat de Bertry's composition visually suggests Rousseau's eminence on par with the Supreme Being—a blasphemous suggestion in the eyes of orthodox Catholics. Jeaurat de Bertry's painting, therefore, hints at a stronger ideological connection to Greco-Roman deification of mortal heroes, rather than Roman Catholic canonization of the saints.

While the cults of dead revolutionary icons undeniably contained Roman Catholic elements, such as association of Marat's preserved heart with the Roman Catholic Sacred Heart of Christ, the parallels between Classical and French hero cults, nonetheless, merit research.[127] The aforementioned knowledge of Saturn, Astraea, Troy, and various Greco-Roman authors certainly opens the possibility of the revolutionaries' awareness of hero cults as a component of pre-Christian Mediterranean religion. The focus on the transformation from mortals to gods through apotheosis scenes further illustrates the issues from espousing solely a Roman Catholic origin hypothesis for revolutionary pantheonization.

CERES-DEMETER AND THE MODERNIZED MYSTERIES

The Eleusinian Mysteries comprised a major part of early ancient Greek religion. Although little is known overall regarding these rites (they were closely guarded secrets of the religion's adherents), Plutarch records that they revolved around the worship of an agrarian mother-goddess figure (Demeter, or Ceres to the Romans) and that women would dress up like

---

[127] Gendron, *The Gilded Youth of Thermidor*, 62.

the goddess for the ceremony.[128] As mentioned previously in this study, *philosophes* such as

Voltaire believed that the ancient mystery religions were more "rational" than Christianity. This

endorsement by Enlightenment thinkers, plus Plutarch's account of the ancient rituals, would

make the Mysteries a strong candidate for the secular cults inspiration in the eyes of the

revolutionary leaders.

An important fact regarding the gods and goddesses of ancient Greek pantheon Plutarch

highlights is that the Greek gods were basically the same as the Egyptian gods.[129] Thus, the

worship of Demeter in the Eleusinian Mysteries was, theologically speaking, the same as

worshipping the Egyptian mother-goddess Isis. In fact, Diderot's *Encyclopédie* explicitly states

this connection to Isis as well in the discussion of Ceres's role as a wheat goddess.[130]

In both the Classical and Egyptian worldviews, the mother goddess figure was associated

with Virgo.[131] The ancient world's religious systems typically lacked unified mythological

narratives and also welcomed syncretism, so Virgo became associated with divinities besides

Astraea. Through the millennia, "astronomical poems and commentators" described Virgo as

wielding an ear of corn, "suggest[ing] that she must be Ceres," the agricultural mother goddess,

while others also claimed Virgo had ties to the moon and the goddess Isis.[132] As the Greco-

Roman world became more syncretized with Egyptian beliefs, Classical culture connected Isis to

Virgo, focusing especially on her role as the god Horus's divine mother and depicting her

---

[128] Ozouf, *Festivals and the French Revolution* 207.
Nilsson, *Greek Popular Religion*, 42, 59, 63.

[129] Plutarch, *Isis and Osiris*, trans. Frank Cole Babbitt, (Loeb Classical Library, 1978), 148.

[130]"Wheat," *The Encyclopedia of Diderot & d'Alembert Collaborative Translation Project*, trans. Robert H. Ketchum (Ann Arbor: MPublishing, University of Michigan Library, 2013). http://hdl.handle.net/2027/spo.did2222.0000.829 (accessed March 20, 2014). Originally published as "Blé," *Encyclopédie ou Dictionnaire raisonné des sciences, des arts et des métiers*, 2:280 (Paris, 1752).

[131] Theony Conos, *Star Myths of the Greeks and Romans: A Sourcebook* (Grand Rapids, Michigan: Phanes Press, 1997), 205.

[132] Frances Yates, *Astraea*, (New York: Routledge, 1999), 32.

bearing the *spica* (the ear of corn or wheat).[133] During the Middles Ages, examples of Virgo-Ceres appeared upon major sites of France, such as the zodiac quatrefoils upon Amiens Cathedral's exterior, which depict Virgo as a shy maiden holding Ceres' signature *spica*.[134] Upon Chartres Cathedral's stained glass of the months and zodiac, Virgo's tondo portrays the maiden holding two plants as she stands across the tondo of summer wheat threshing, a nod to the connection between the constellation's personification and cereal agriculture.[135] Such syncretism of the mother goddesses with Virgo-Astraea would account for why a constellation, whose name translates to "virgin," would become ironically associated with the great mother archetype of Ceres/Demeter/Isis during antiquity.[136] As Frances Yates noted in her study of this antique virgin-mother astronomical symbol in Elizabethan England, "The just virgin is thus a complex character, fertile and barren at the same time; orderly and righteous, yet tinged with [Isis's] oriental moon-ecstasies."[137] Like many aspects France during the Terror, this astral goddess of the Golden Age's attributes contradicted themselves.

In *Politics, Culture, and Class in the French Revolution*, Hunt correctly states that Reason/Liberty's[138] form as Marianne was a personification of the Republic designed to take the place of the Virgin Mary. Hunt's statement is true, but not fully carved in the round. While Marianne operated as a new divine feminine figure for the people to fixate upon, she was not

---

[133] Tim Hegedus, *Early Christianity and Ancient Astrology* (New York: Peter Lang Publishing, 2007), 237.

[134] Stuart Whatling, "Amiens Cathedral West Façade – the 'Zodiac/Months' Quatrefoils," *The Corpus of Medieval Art*, http://www.medievalart.org.uk/Amiens/West_Facade/ZodiacMonths/AmiensWest_Quatrefoil_ZodiacMonths_Key.htm (accessed January 10, 2014).

[135] Whatling, "Labours of the Months/Signs of the Zodiac," *The Corpus of Medieval Art* http://www.medievalart.org.uk/chartres/028a_pages/Chartres_Bay028a_key.htm (accessed January 10, 2014).

[136] Yates, *Astraea*, 32-33.

[137] Ibid., 33.

[138] The goddess figures of Reason, Liberty, Marianne, Nature, Victory, etc., were virtually interchangeable, as Hunt points out in her chapter, "Symbolic Forms of Political Culture," in *Politics, Culture, and Class in the French Revolution*.

merely a neo-Marian figure, but a refashioning of the divine feminine worshipped long before

the advent of Mariology: the many-named, paradoxical virgin-mother earth goddess living in the

stars—Isis, Demeter-Ceres, Astraea. When a local beauty queen, selected for her moral

reputation and family background, draped herself in a *chiton* as a symbolic proxy for the goddess

of Reason in the *Fête* of Reason, this practice did not mirror Marian devotional practices, but the

Mysteries' rituals surrounding the drama of Demeter-Ceres and her daughter Persephone.[139]

Other imagery of Ceres-Demeter manifested in Revolutionary culture. Jean Jacques

Lagrenée's illustration of the *Declaration des droits de l'homme et du citoyen* places Ceres,

holding wheat, bundles atop the Mosaic-style tablets as she sits across from the personification

of the French Republic (identified by her Liberty cap and Gallic rooster).[140] One anonymous

engraving of *Raison* (printed circa 1793-1794) depicted her enthroned and wielding a torch made

of a flaming sheaf, instead of the usual fasces-like torch.[141] More curiously, there exists an

anonymous design for a chariot of Ceres, presumably for the Festival of the Supreme Being's

procession.[142] Portraying Ceres surrounded by bundles of wheat and backed by a tree (perhaps a

Liberty Tree, although it is difficult to be sure), this drawing suggests that, around 1794, *fête*

designers intended *Cerès* to be explicitly present in the Deistic Cult of the Supreme Being.

Besides these manifestations of the agricultural goddess in two-dimensional works of art, French

women during the Directory could even purchase "tunics *à la Cerès*" (as well as other Greco-

---

[139] Lyttle, "Deistic Piety in the Cults of the French Revolution," 23.
McManners, *The French Revolution and the Church*, 102.
Ozouf, *Festivals and the French Revolution*, 101.
Nilsson, *Greek Popular Religion*, 42, 59, 63.
[140] Jean Jacques Lagrenée, *Declaration des droits de l'homme et du citoyen : présentée au people français par la Convention nationale, le 24 juin et acceptée le 10 août 1793 23 fervidor* [sic] *l'an 1ᵉʳ de la République une & indivisible*, engraving design, 1793, Bibliothèque nationale de France, Paris.
[141] *Raison*, colored engraving, ca. 1793-1794, Bibliothèque nationale de France, Paris.
[142] *Char de Cerès pour la fête de l'Etre Suprême*, black crayon and pen drawing, 1794, Bibliothèque nationale de France, Paris.

Roman-inspired garb, such as Greek *corthurnus* sandals), in keeping with the period's latest fashion trends.[143]

While Ceres' presence was not always as explicit as *le char de Cerès* or Lagrenée's *Declaration,*[144] her imagery is noteworthy, because of her association with the Eleusinian Mysteries (which the likes of Voltaire favored to the rituals of the Gallican Church), as well as her deeply entrenched ties to Astraea-Virgo and Isis, both of whom also featured in the revolutionary cults composite mythologies.

WHY IS ISIS THE ONLY EGYPTIAN DEITY FEATURED IN A REPUBLICAN *FÊTE?*

Given the First Republic's desire to return to the "more natural" religious traditions of antiquity it would appear odd that fêtes favor more of a Greco-Roman aesthetic Isis and other Egyptian imagery did not feature more heavily in the First Republic's neo-paganism. The reason the French did not take a more Egyptian route with regard to crafting their cultic iconography comes from the fact that they little beyond Plutarch as their source regarding the religion of the ancient Egyptians.[145] Their other source came from Court de Gébelin's and the *Encyclopédie's* respective assertions that the ancient Gauls worshipped Isis.[146]

Court de Gébelin based his rationale on his own etymology of the city name "Paris," which he parsed as "Ship of Isis" by claiming that "par" was Celtic for "ship" and that the "-is" came from Isis.[147] He also claimed that Notre Dame in Paris was originally the site of a Druidic

---

[143] Alfred Richard Allinson, *The Days of the Directoire* (New York: John Lane, 1910), 109.

[144] That is, at least according to the current resources available at the time of this research.

[145] Ozouf, *Festivals and the French Revolution,* 273.

[146] Shaw, *Time and French Revolution,* 66-67.

[147] Farley, *A Cultural History of the Tarot,* 102.

E. A. Reynolds-Ball, *Paris in Its Splendor* (Boston: Dana Estes, 1900), 1: 6.

temple to Isis, but this claim does not appear based on hard evidence.[148] The *Encyclopédie*'s

"Paris" article even calls the theory that the French capital was originally dedicated to Isis *"une*

pure fiction."[149] Nonetheless, the question of whether or not Court de Gébelin was a slipshod

etymologist matters little. What matters is that his writings were immensely popular in

eighteenth-century France and that many people would have been familiar with his idea that Isis

was the Parisian "original" deity.

The *Encylcopédie*'s contents, however, were not entirely against the possibility of Isis

worship in ancient France. The "Minerva" article cites Cicero for its theory of potential Gallic

worship of Isis in antiquity.[150] According to Cicero, the Gauls worshipped a form of Isis, but his

understanding of Gallic religion could possibly have been influenced by the *interpretatio romana*

(the Romans' method of understanding foreign deities in terms of their own pantheon).[151] The

Roman historian Tacitus famously applied the *interpretatio romana* to the Germanic pantheon,

claiming that first-century Germans worshiped Mercury, Mars, Hercules, and Isis.[152] As with the

case of Court de Gébelin's etymology, the issue is not the veracity of the *Encyclopédie*'s

assertions. What makes the idea of a Gallic Isis worthy of note is the fact that a publication as

reputable and popular as the *Encyclopédie* spread the idea into Enlightenment France's

---

[148] Farley, *A Cultural History of the Tarot,* 102.

[149] Louis, chevalier de Jaucourt, "Paris," in *Encyclopédie, ou dictionnaire raisonné des sciences, des arts et des métiers, etc.,* eds. Denis Diderot and Jean le Rond d'Alembert. University of Chicago: ARTFL Encyclopédie Project (Spring 2013 Edition), Robert Morrissey (ed.), http://artflsrv02.uchicago.edu/cgi-bin/philologic/getobject.pl?c.10:2854.encyclopedie0513.9770232 (accessed March 1, 2014).

[150] Louis, chevalier de Jaucourt, "Minerva," *The Encyclopedia of Diderot & d'Alembert Collaborative Translation Project,* trans. Gabriela Jasin (Ann Arbor: MPublishing, University of Michigan Library, 2005), http://hdl.handle.net/2027/spo.did2222.0000.392 (accessed March 22, 2014). Originally published as "Minerve," *Encyclopédie ou Dictionnaire raisonné des sciences, des arts et des métiers,* 10:544 (Paris, 1765).

[151] Clifford Ando, *"Interpretatio Romana," Classical Philology* 100, No. 1 (January 2005): 41. Jaucourt, "Minerva."

[152] Tacitus, *The Agricola and Germania,* trans. A. J. Church and W. J. Brodribb (London: Macmillan, 1877), Internet Medieval Sourcebook, http://www.fordham.edu/halsall/source/tacitus1.html (accessed March 2, 2014).

intellectual atmosphere. The idea that the inhabitants of ancient France worshipped deities from

the Mediterranean, therefore, would not seem unbelievable to the well-read Frenchmen, and her

presence in the new regime would not be shocking to readers of Court de Gébelin or the

Encyclopédie.

No matter Isis's supposed importance to the ancient French as their "original" goddess,

she did not become as omnipresent in the *fêtes* and Republican ephemera as Liberty or Reason,

because the French, during the Enlightenment, still possessed relatively little knowledge of

ancient Egyptian religion. Despite the records of various Roman historians, the ancient Egyptians

had yet to regain their own voice in history, because the French did not discover the Rosetta

Stone until 1799.[153] This lack of Egyptian resources explains why David crafted a huge statue of

Isis lactating[154] to represent Nature at the *fête* dedicated to the constitution's unveiling, yet did

not incorporate explicitly Egyptian motifs much beyond that bizarre cameo.[155] The few other

overt representations of Isis during the Revolution are memorabilia of the statue to

commemorate her unveiling at the Constitution's *fête*, such as print illustrations of the event

(e.g., *La Fontaine de la Régénération* illustration by Charles Monnet) and upon the obverse of

the five-décimes coin minted in Year II.[156]

---

[153] "The Rosetta Stone," *The British Museum*,
http://www.britishmuseum.org/explore/highlights/highlight_objects/aes/t/the_rosetta_stone.aspx
(accessed 21 April 2012).

[154] The statue's bare breasts actually functioned and spurt forth water to the crowds. See
Edelstein's *The Terror of Natural Right* for further details about the *Fête* of the Constitution.

[155] Edelstein, *Terror of Natural Right*, 184.

[156] Charles Monnet, *La Fontaine de la régénération, sur les débris de la Bastille, le 10 août 1793*,
engraving, 1796, Bibliothèque nationale de France, Paris.

Shaw, *Time and the French Revolution*, 67-68.

LIBERTY TREES: THE MAYPOLE REINCARNATED

Agrarian worship did not figure only in the Eleusinian Mysteries. Bacchanlia were raucous parties and processions of worship dedicated to agricultural deities, like the viticultural god Dionysus.[157] One element of the worship of Bacchus/Dionysus entailed worship around a holy tree or maypole/-bough, called a *bacchos*.[158] These holy poles/trees were symbolic of the phallus and sometimes also associated with Apollo.[159] According to Plutarch, holy trees also figured into the worship of the Egyptian god Osiris (Isis's husband): "all who reverence Osiris are prohibited from destroying a cultivated tree or blocking up a spring of water."[160]

Initially, revolutionaries planted liberty trees as celebratory maypoles, or sometimes as signs of rebellion against the *ancien régime*.[161] "By May of 1792, 60,000 liberty trees had been planted in France."[162] Eventually these trees gained their own rituals and regulations.[163] Designed to take the place of the cross in town squares across France after the cross became an outlawed symbol (because it was a "sign of superstition"), town officials planted these trees as a community event with great pomp and ceremony.[164]

After dechristianization began, however, liberty trees became religious symbols of new regime France and its "natural" beliefs. Designed to take the place of the cross in town squares across France after the cross became an outlawed symbol (because it was a "sign of superstition"), town officials planted these trees as a community event with great pomp and

---

[157] Nilsson, *Greek Popular Religion*, 36.

[158] Ibid., 39.

[159] Ibid., 36, 39.

[160] Plutarch, *Isis and Osiris*, 88.

[161] Ozouf, *Festivals and the French Revolution*, 256.

[162] Lynn Hunt, "Engravings," in *The French Revolution: Conflicting Interpretations*, 5th ed., ed. by Frank A. Kafker, James M. Laux, and Darline Gay Levy (Malabar, Florida: Krieger Publishing, 2002), 271.

[163] Hunt, *Politics, Culture, and Class in the French Revolution*, 59.

[164] Ozouf, *Festivals and the French Revolution*, 225, 254, 260-261.

ceremony.[165] Like the maypole/-bough of early Greece, the Liberty tree became associated with the "rhythms of human life" and masculinity in Revolutionary France.[166] Townspeople reacted to Liberty trees with great awe and reverence: "they knelt in front of the tree, they put their arms around the trunk and kissed it, touched it several times in order to receive its beneficent powers."[167] In Amiens, when the local Liberty tree died, the people covered themselves in black and carried the dead tree in a funeral procession.[168] Liberty trees, therefore, illustrated elements of both ancient tree worship, like that documented of Osiris's followers, as well as the maypole/*bacchos* traditions from Greece.[169]

The strong connection of the French to the liberty trees is not surprising, though, considering the French long utilized maypoles/may-trees for rural, peasant folk celebrations as "symbols of communal solidarity," such as May Day festivities.[170] In Mayenne, for example, rural peasants would celebrate the first day of May by planting a small tree, besides other festivities such as singing May carols.[171] Residents of Brie also erected may-trees in the town square, which they would top with a floral wreath.[172] The maypole is a particularly iconic element of Celto-Breton culture.[173] "Sacred trees" (i.e., maypoles) from Bretagne's pre-Christian Druidic tradition were the literal centerpieces in Breton churches.[174] Maypoles were so ingrained in Breton culture during the seventeenth and eighteenth centuries that Breton colonists

---

[165] Ibid.

[166] Ibid., 257.

[167] Ibid., 254.

[168] Ibid., 259.

[169] Ibid., 232, 257.

[170] J. David Harden, "Liberty Caps and Liberty Trees," *Past & Present*, no. 146 (February 1995): 68.

[171] James George Frazer, *The Golden Bough* (Macmillan, 1922), 146. Kindle edition.

[172] Ibid., 151.

[173] Benson, "Breton and Muslim Antecedents in Vodou Drapo," 72.

[174] Alfred Métraux, *Voodoo in Haiti*, 2nd ed., trans. by Hugo Charteris (New York: Schocken Books, 1974), 81.

transplanted them to Saint-Domingue, where Vodou practitioners adopted them into their own

Mardi Gras-style holiday, Karneval.[175]

Liberty trees, therefore, illustrated both ancient tree worship, like that documented of

Osiris's followers, as well as following the local maypole traditions stemming from Celto-French

folk culture.[176]

CONCLUSION: ANALYZING THE REVOLUTIONARY CULTS BEYOND POLITICAL SYMBOLISM AND THE APPROPRIATION OF ROMAN CATHOLICISM

As the motifs from Greco-Roman mytho-history and religion, astrology, and Celtic

France have illustrated, the revolutionary state cults and their imagery were the outcome of a

culture raised on Classical works and possessed a penchant for heterodoxy and the Occult. While

an increasing number of studies explore the festivals and the cultic symbolism of the Republic,

few delve into the blend of heterodoxy and preference for Greco-Roman antiquity that made the

state cults conceivable, and, therefore, possible.

Through the analysis of symbolism of the Astraea's role in the mythical Golden Age of

Saturn, the historical discourse of the goddess moves beyond viewing the state cults' imagery as

appropriations of the Virgin Mary. While Astraea does maintain links to the virgin-mother

archetype à la Mary, claiming that virgin-mother types with variations on the name "Mary," does

not provide a fully rounded understanding of the Revolution's rich symbolism and ignores the

desire of the *fêtes'* designers to create a pre-Christian, naturalistic religion for the new regime.

Astraea's fluid ties to primal, agricultural deities Ceres-Demeter and Isis would aid in creating

the theoretical religious system of idyllic pre-history.

---

[175] Benson, "Some Breton and Muslim Antecedents of Vodou Drapo," 72.
[176] Ibid., 232, 257.

Likewise, the Roman Catholic lens does not fully account for all elements of the pantheonized hero cults, since saints do not undergo apotheosization in Catholic iconography. In fact, the Catholic appropriation argument cannot account for the strong reception of liberty trees throughout France. Only through an understanding of Classicalism and pre-Christian, French folk religious practices can the origins of revolutionary tree veneration come to light.

CONCLUSION

Although current cultural trends arguably indicate that the West is entering the post-Christian era, orthodox Christianity still serves as a cultural lens in understanding Western religious images and practices. The French Revolution's religious motifs and imagery, however, borrowed beyond the sponsored religion of the *ancien régime*. To understand the cults, historians must understand the complications surrounding France's eighteenth-century intellectual and religious culture.

Studying the Classics has been a mainstay of Western education since recorded history. During the Enlightenment, French philosophers viewed Classical civilization as the key to unraveling the historical "truth" beyond the "superstitious" biblical narrative of humanity. Rousseau idealized the Spartans and called for mankind's return to his ancient, "natural state." Greco-Roman practices, such as the Eleusinian Mysteries, predated the advent of Christianity, so Voltaire and other influential Enlightenment thinkers viewed these ancient pagan beliefs and rituals as inherently more "rational" than those of the Church. As revolutionary leaders such as Robespierre avidly read the works of Enlightenment *philosophes,* these ideas of "natural" beliefs versus "superstition" would shape the worldview of the Revolution.

France's fascination with the Occult and magic also shaped the revolutionary worldview. Although this was the "Age of Reason," esotericist Antoine Court de Gébelin was just as popular as Rousseau.[1] While officially banning all religions beyond that promoted by the Gallican Church, Enlightenment France's populace exhibited a wide range of heterodoxy, from dabbling in prophetic literature to hiring renegade priests. This fascination with divination, prophetic seers, papally condemned Freemasonry, and other Occult interests exhibits that many French

---

[1] Edelstein, *The Terror of Natural Right,* 246.

never fully practiced orthodox Roman Catholicism. This relaxed view the French took toward Church dogma would make the revolutionary cults possible: heterodoxy is a slippery slope that makes apostasy eventually palatable.

The combination of Classicalism and Occult-infused heterodoxy made the acceptance of the anti-Christian state cults possible. Although it would be a gross generalization to assert that every single Frenchmen was in favor of the government-mandated religious changes, the fact that enough citizens participated in the Festival of the Supreme Being to fill up Champs-de-Mars, as depicted in Pierre-Antoine Demanchy's iconic image, clarifies that plenty found at least relative contentment with the religious decisions instituted by the Republic.[2] Analyzing key cult elements—the goddess figures, Phrygian cap, pantheonized heroes, and liberty trees—within the aforementioned Classical-Occult paradigm enables a fuller understanding of these eccentric years in the young republic better than merely adhering to a simplistic formula that the cult designers crafted, say, the image of Marianne only as an alterative to the Virgin Mary. The literary and artistic records speak otherwise: the French revolutionary cults imposed a complex system of ancient Greco-Roman symbolism married with Occult arts, especially astrology.

As the historiography continues to grow, more insight shall shine on these short, eccentric years during the Revolution. Hopefully more historians shall join in fleshing out this branch of French Revolutionary studies sooner rather than later. As mentioned at the start of this study, today's general public is hungry for exciting, eccentric historical narratives, hence Americans' fascination with the Nazis' SS cults, Himmler's feudal hunt for the Aryan Atlantis, and other fantastic, yet true tales. Although academia at large has yet to explore the "dark side" of French Revolution (i.e., the antique, Occult influences in the cults), an infinite number of self-

---

[2] Pierre-Anotine Demanchy, *Le Fête de l'Etre suprême au Champ-de-Mars (20 prairial an II - 8 juin 1794)*, 1794, Musée Carnavelet, Paris.

appointed historians and researchers on the Internet are creating content on the subject—unfortunately, the hoards of Reddit, Above Top Secret, Disinfo, and other discussion forums promote assertions in the conspiratorial spirit of the abbé Barruel. As these (generally) well-meaning promoters of sensationalized half-truths and outright myths dispel their misinformation into the fathomless depths of the Internet, more and more users begin to believe the over-simplistic untruths (e.g., "a Freemasonic conspiracy of the Revolution" as "evidenced" by a goddess figure holding fasces). Historians need to step in and properly educate these hungry minds in search of an interesting story, lest they have more than their share of work trying to reeducate the ill-informed who "read something online."

For now, however, this work's study of the revolutionary cults aims to pave the way for more, in-depth analyses of the French Revolutionary cults that move beyond the paradigm that the much of the imagery stemmed from merely appropriating Roman Catholic elements, and instead deal with the eccentricities like the Golden Age of Saturn.